ST ANDREWS LINKS

St Andrews Links

Six Centuries of Golf

TOM JARRETT
AND PETER MASON

FOREWORD BY JACK NICKLAUS

EDINBURGH AND LONDON

Frontispiece: The Links, the town and The Castle Course on the far headland

This edition, 2009

Copyright © Tom Jarrett, 1995
New and updated material © Peter Mason, 2009

First published in Great Briain in 1995 by
MAINSTREAM PUBLISHING COMPANY
(EDINBURGH) LTD
7 Albany Street
Edinburgh EH1 3UG

ISBN 9781845965013

Reprinted 2002, 2004

The publisher would like to thank St Andrews Links Trust
for its co-operation and support in producing this book

Photographs credited to the George Washington
Wilson Collection have been reproduced with the
permission of Aberdeen University Library (ref. A123)

Text design by Gill McColl

A catalogue record for this book is available
from the British Library

Typeset in Baskerville and OptimusPrinceps

Printed in Great Britain by
Butler Tanner & Dennis Ltd, Frome, Somerset

CONTENTS

PREFACE

The decision to write this book was not entirely my own. My great friend and colleague, press photographer George Cowie, and I used to meet from time to time in the New Golf Club, and inevitably the conversation would turn to golf and St Andrews Links. Neither George nor I could boast much proficiency at the game, but golf and the Links formed a large part of our stock-in-trade as professional men.

My first contact with the Links was made almost as soon as I was big enough to tote a bag of golf clubs – in those days the average set contained about seven clubs. I acted as a boy caddie on Saturdays and during school holidays. This helped me to go back to school with a new suit of clothes, a new pair of boots – and a healthy tan.

During that time I learned a lot about the Links and its turbulent history from the older caddies. They were a mixed bunch – there were a few dropouts, but a large proportion were old seafaring men who had found it difficult to earn a living from the receding fishing industry and had turned to the Links to earn what they could to eke out their savings. They were intelligent, fiercely independent men, and they were always willing to talk to a youngster who was patient enough to listen to their tales.

This experience as a caddie was of some help when I left school with my Highers in 1932 – right in the middle of the industrial depression. University grants were almost non-existent – as were career jobs – so all that was left was to register as a licensed caddie. At this time, any person who earned his livelihood from a golf-related activity was reckoned to have lost his amateur status, so technically I had become a professional golfer before I was even a competent amateur. In 1937 the opportunity presented itself to me to enter journalism as a freelance, and for the next 43 years I reported on the golfing and community scene in and around St Andrews.

George Cowie often urged me to write a history of the Links, and, indeed, he provided me with a large number of photographic prints from his personal collection. I am pleased now to have written something of which George would perhaps have approved.

Many others have helped, particularly the staff of St Andrews University Library, who have always been able to point me in the right direction. Bob Smart, keeper of the muniments at St Andrews University, has gone out of his way to help, and I have been much encouraged by local historians Dr R.G. Cant and Gordon Christie. The facilities for research provided by the Hay Fleming Reference Library in St Andrews have also been invaluable.

Tom Jarrett

FOREWORD

St Andrews Links is steeped in the history, lore and legends of the game of golf. Indeed, for many centuries the history of the game was made on the Links. So I was delighted when asked to contribute to this book, which traces the full extent of that storied history.

The Links at St Andrews is unique in the world of golf, wrapped in the memories of the giants of the game – past and present – and an atmosphere of timelessness that seems to pervade every corner of the town.

My introduction to the Old Course came in 1964 when, at the age of 24, I fell in love with it the first time I played it. My feelings for this extraordinary golf location have been reinforced on every visit. Yet my Open Championship wins in 1970 and 1978, and my final Championship round in 2005, perfectly punctuated with a birdie on the last hole, have been particularly memorable. I deliberately chose St Andrews as the venue at which to conclude my major championship career because of its place in the game of golf and its place in history, as well as what it has meant to me personally. Not only have I been fortunate to enjoy success here, but I have also always felt a special bond with the Scots and the people of St Andrews, and it is as if they have adopted me as one of their own. I was also privileged and humbled to receive a doctorate from the University of St Andrews, as well as memberships of the Royal and Ancient Golf Club and the St Andrews Golf Club. In 2000, I was delighted to be presented with the Freedom of the Links. All of these honours and moments have served to strengthen my feeling for, and close association with, the town and its golf community.

Part of what makes the courses at St Andrews Links so special in the world of golf is that they are open to the public. As this book makes clear, that public access has been defended vigorously over many centuries by the St Andrews golf community, so that to this day any golfer may play on the Links and non-golfers can go for a stroll to watch them. The caretakers of the game realise that to grow the game we need to give people the opportunity to enjoy the venues on which golf's history was written and allow them to embrace the game's past while ensuring its future.

The story that is told here highlights the townspeople's love of the game and the Links – a love that I hope you come to share, as I do, when you play the courses. I hope that reading this book will give you a greater insight into why St Andrews Links holds such a unique place in golfers' hearts all over the world. Just as it does in mine.

Jack Nicklaus

LEFT: Jack Nicklaus
(Jim Mandeville/Nicklaus Design)

INTRODUCTION

This chronicle has been written for the purpose of putting on record the events and discourses which led up to the re-acquisition of the golf links by St Andrews Town Council, to illustrate the fervour with which the people of St Andrews have defended their rights, and to trace the physical development of the historic Links. It is also intended to highlight the partnership between the town of St Andrews and the Royal and Ancient Golf Club – a partnership which has existed under statute since 1894, and on a voluntary basis for very much longer.

It is not intended to dwell on the origins and history of the game of golf, for this has been examined and re-examined by historians of many nationalities, usually without any definitive outcome. Nor is it intended to ponder over the mediaeval charters which confirmed the patrimonial rights of the townspeople of St Andrews, for those have already been explained at length by that distinguished historian Dr Hay Fleming, by Dr J.B. Salmond whose *Story of the R&A* is ranked with the modern golf classics, and by J.K. Robertson in his *St Andrews – Home of Golf*. Liberty will be taken, however, to touch on these briefly, for no account of the history of St Andrews would be complete without some reference to them.

There has been a vacuum in knowledge of the Links between the date of their re-acquisition in 1894 and entry into the twenty-first century. The 114-year period between the first Act in 1894 and 2008 has seen two bursts of intensive development of the Links, and these have been chronicled here, along with some of the controversies that they caused. The fluctuating fortunes of that period have tested almost to the limit the partnership between the town and the R&A. The partnership has, nevertheless, endured because it has been based on trust and has been characterised by the willingness of the partners to help one another in times of difficulty. In places, this relationship will be explored in some detail, since it is important to know not only what decisions were taken but also to understand the thinking behind those decisions.

LEFT: The famous view (Russell Kirk)
OVERLEAF: The R&A Clubhouse

I

THE BEGINNINGS

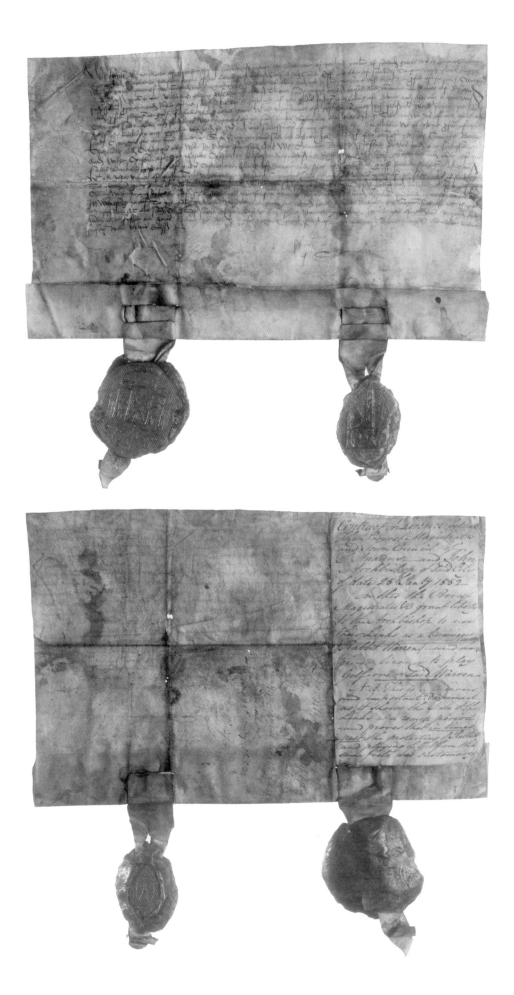

Contract of Lease between
the Provost Magistrates
and Town Council and John
Andrews and John
Strathbuck of Leith
of Aite 25th Jun ... 1552

... this the Provost
Magistrates ... grant Charter
to their Son Bishop to own
their Lands as a Coney ...
Rabbit Warren ... and a
... licence to ... the
Golf ... and ... Warren

... it is ... and
important Document
as it shows the date the
Lands ... a long period
and ... that in time
past ... protecting Rabbits
and ... of it from the
same ... the customary ...

EARLY GOLF AT ST ANDREWS

The Links form a peninsula lying north and west of the town of St Andrews. Most of the area was reclaimed from the sea, first by natural processes, and later with the help of man, using sand-binding grasses like marram and sea lyme which assist in the formation of sand dunes.

The land reclaimed was poor and unproductive, and it was used in the early days for the grazing of sheep, which thrived on the short, sea-washed grasses. Sand holes and whin bushes provided shelter for man and beast.

An important factor in the development of the Links was that the harbour or port of St Andrews was in the estuary of the River Eden, which forms part of the northern boundary of the Links. It was to this port that merchants from the Netherlands came to trade with the Scots. They came to St Andrews because, as the mediaeval ecclesiastical capital of Scotland, it was the most important city in the country. These merchants, mostly Dutch and Flemish, played a version of their own stick-and-ball game called *kolven*. The St Andrews shepherds doubtless had their own stick-and-ball game, hitting at loose stones with their crooks. They may have picked up something from the Dutch and Flemish game – even if it was only a version of the name.

It is impossible to make any incontrovertible claim about the origins of golf. The game just evolved, developing its own individuality and traditions, much like the Links which it graces and the sand dunes which give it the dignity and the rugged grandeur that set it apart from other forms of sport and sports arenas.

There is no doubt about the popularity of the game. James II banned the playing of golf and football by an Act of 1457 because he felt that young men were wasting their time at sport instead of developing their martial skills at the archery butts. James III repeated the prohibition in 1471 and so did James IV in 1492. The latter obviously found it a frustrating business, and in 1502 he took up golf. His first set of clubs cost 14 shillings – 70 pence in decimal currency – and, ironically, they were made by a bow-maker. King James VI settled the golf-versus-archery conflict, for in 1603 he succeeded to the English throne and moved to London with his court, which included a number of golfers who practised their game on Blackheath Common.

LEFT: Archbishop Hamilton's Charter, which confirmed the rights of the townspeople to play golf on the Links. It was lost for some years and in 1994 was unearthed in a cupboard in the basement of the Town Hall. The archbishop's and the town's seals are still attached. The charter's main purpose was to allow the archbishop to farm rabbits on the Links. Several centuries later, physical damage caused by rabbits led to conflict between landowners and the townspeople

THE CHARTERS

The rights of the people of St Andrews on the Links are firmly rooted in charters granted by monarchs and Church leaders. In 1123, the area of the Links was granted to the Burgh of St Andrews by a charter of King David. At that time there was no reference to golf, and it seems likely that the Links were used as a source of peat for fuel, turf for roofs and rabbits for food.

The first mention of golfing rights is in the charter granted by Archbishop John Hamilton in 1552, in which he confirmed, ratified and approved the right of the community, among other things, in 'playing at golff, futball, schuteing at all gamis with all uther manner of pastyme as ever thai pleis'. Hamilton's charter was confirmed by Archbishop Gladstanes in 1614.

The Hamilton charter was drawn up principally to establish the archbishop's right to run the Links as a rabbit warren. Rabbits provided both food and clothing, and under the charter, which made an agreement with the town authorities legally binding, the archbishop was entitled to all the rabbits from the Links. The references to the townspeople's rights of access and pastimes defined the limits of his authority over the ground.

While the various charters confirmed the rights of the people of St Andrews to play golf over the Links, it is probable that the right was established by use and wont long before the charters were granted. The burgh authorities were permitted to let or lease parts of the Links, but they were careful always to include safeguards for the protection of the golfing areas. For example, in September 1726, when William Gib, Deacon of the Baxters (Bakers), was allowed to put his black-and-white rabbits on the Links, it was conditional that 'the links are not to be spoiled where the golfing is used'.

Another such instance was in 1769, when the Town Council exchanged more than six acres of land for a similar plot owned by the Laird of Strathtyrum. The laird made a condition 'that the part of the links as presently golfed upon shall be kept entire and not ploughed up'. This reservation was imposed on the purchasers of the Links some years later.

II

THE TOWN
AND THE CLUB

THE R&A

The history of the Royal and Ancient Golf Club has been recorded many times, and this account is not intended to be regarded as comprehensive. The history of the club, however, has been woven through the Links from the very day of its foundation as the Society of St Andrews Golfers on 14 May 1754, and no history of the Links would be complete without a significant section devoted to golf's ruling body.

Golf has been Scotland's national game since the Middle Ages. It was played by the highest and the lowest in the land wherever a piece of waste ground was available. It received a tremendous boost in the upper echelons of society in 1502 when King James IV of Scotland took up the game. In those early days, golf and archery were popular sporting activities, and it is significant that James IV's clubs were made for him by a bow-maker in Perth.

As more and more people took up the game, the urge to pit one's skill against another's led to the formation of societies or clubs whose main object was to arrange golf meetings.

In 1754, 22 gentlemen, mainly peers, landowners, university professors and local dignitaries from Fife, formed the Society of St Andrews Golfers. It is unlikely that these gentlemen had a spontaneous and unprompted urge to bind themselves into a golfing fraternity with St Andrews Links as their base; it is more likely that, having played over the Links for many years, they felt they ought to have a corporate identity, for they were not the first to form themselves into a golfing society. The Honourable Company of Edinburgh Golfers had been formed at Leith ten years earlier, and the Royal Burgess Society of Edinburgh claims to have been founded even earlier.

The 22 members of the St Andrews society marked their foundation by playing for a silver club bearing the cross of St Andrew over a course of 22 holes – 11 out, and the same 11 back. The rules – 13 of them – were borrowed from the Honourable Company with one minor change.

It was agreed in May 1776 that the members should meet once a fortnight for golf and for dinner, which was served in Glass's Inn at the corner of South Castle Street and South Street. It was not, however, their only '19th hole', for they changed inns from time to time. It is also on record that the society held its annual ball in the Tolbooth, or town hall, which stood in Market Street between Logies Lane and Muttoes Lane.

LEFT: Detail from picture on page 21

19

Putting out in front of the clubhouse. Note the starter's box on wheels and, in the right foreground, the Valley of Sin (George Washington Wilson Collection)

In 1817, a substantial contribution was made to St Andrews Town Council towards the improvement of the town hall, and in recognition of this the society was entitled to use the Upper Hall for its spring and autumn meetings. In October 1856, the council was in the process of building a new town hall. The R&A made a contribution of £50 towards the cost, on the condition that the club would continue to have the right to use the building, and the annual dinner was held there every year until 2002, when the event became too big even for the town hall.

The name of the society was changed to the Royal and Ancient Golf Club of St Andrews in 1834. The monarch at that time was King William IV, who also held the title Duke of St Andrews, and the society invited him to become their patron and asked his permission to change the society's title. King William agreed, and a year or two later, he presented the club with a medal known as the King William IV Medal, to be contested as a perpetual challenge trophy.

It was in that same year that Sir Hugh Lyon Playfair came to live in St Andrews, having retired from the army. He played a leading part in the foundation of the Union Club, which, although predominantly an archers' club, had a room in its clubhouse set aside for the use of golfers, for the club had its own 'Union Parlour'. This building occupied a site where the red-stone Hamilton Hall now stands overlooking the 18th green of the Old Course and only a sizeable downhill putt to where the R&A Clubhouse now stands.

The Union Club, having the advantage of its own clubhouse, prospered. This may have had something to do with the friendship which developed between the members of the two clubs. By 1853 the Union Club had developed to such an extent that it was proposed that a new clubhouse be built on land lying to the east of what is now the first teeing ground of the Old Course, and which the Town Council had promised to make available to the Society of Golfers 33 years earlier.

In October 1853, the Union Club agreed that the Royal and Ancient Golf Club and the Union Club should be united, and in the following year the R&A passed a similar resolution, but it was not until 1877 that the two bodies became fully integrated under the title of the senior partner, the Royal and Ancient Golf Club of St Andrews. It appears that in the years between 1854 and 1877 each club retained its own identity, each keeping its own minute book. The single constitution for the amalgamated club was adopted in May 1877. Workmen carried out their duties swiftly in the mid-nineteenth century, for the foundation stone of the new clubhouse was laid in June 1853 and the first meeting of the Union Club was held there on 19 July of the following year.

The acquisition of the land on which the new clubhouse was built resulted from a piece of horse-trading between the Society of St Andrews Golfers and the Town Council in October 1820. At about that time, the Town Council was feuing land – effectively selling, but with a continuing ground rent – to the south of the first and 18th fairways of the Old Course. This land, lying between what became Pilmour Links and Links Road, was regarded by the society as part of the golfing ground, and they objected to its alienation for other purposes. Their threat of action was taken so seriously by the council that they came to an understanding with the society. If the society withdrew their opposition, the council would make available at some future date a piece of ground lying to the east of the first teeing area on which the society might build a clubhouse.

The Duke of York, later King George VI, playing in as captain of the R&A in September 1930, watched by Andra' Kirkaldy and Col. P.G.M. Skene, the outgoing captain, and a large crowd (D.C. Thomson)

This arrangement between the club and the council was mirrored in the late 1850s by a further agreement. Until that time, the town's lifeboat was housed in a building alongside the 18th fairway of the Old Course. It was kept there because in those days, when ships relied mainly on sail, they were often trapped in St Andrews Bay and were blown into trouble at the West Sands. The lifeboat was then trundled across the 18th and first fairways and manhandled into the sea. Several important rescues were effected there over the years. But after a while, the lifeboat house was moved to the East Sands, and the building beside the Links became redundant. The Town Council wanted to sell a small area of land to the west of the lifeboat house and eastwards from the Swilcan Burn in order 'to make a proper termination to the range of houses called Gibson Place', and they asked the club not to object to the proposal. The council's concern was that the land bounding the golfing ground was a very sensitive area. This is brought out by the R&A Committee's reply to the council, in which it was stated:

It appears from the minutes of the club dated 6 February 1824 that when the club consented to the erection of the lifeboat house, they did so on the express condition that in case, at any future time, the house should cease to be appropriated to the purpose of keeping a lifeboat, the ground whereon it is built should revert to and become part of the golfing course over which the servitude of golfing extends. There is no doubt therefore that the club could insist that if the building ceases to be used for the purpose for which it was erected (which is now intended) the site of it should be restored to the golf course. There is equally little doubt that the club might prevent the Town Council from feuing any additional piece of ground adjoining the site.

Having made their position clear, the club adopted a bargaining posture in which they proposed to offer no objection 'since the house was to have a neat elevation in harmony with the building already erected'. They withheld objection to the sale, or feu, but added 'if the club should find it necessary to obtain from the Town Council any additional ground for the enlargement of the clubhouse, the council should offer all reasonable facility for the club doing so'.

ABOVE LEFT:
Inside the R&A's safe
(Masakuni Akiyama)

ABOVE RIGHT:
The R&A 'Big Room'
(Masakuni Akiyama)

The R&A took advantage of the situation in 1872 when they submitted plans for an extension of the clubhouse by adding two rooms to the north side and progressed in their plans by taking a feu of ground at the rate of £2 10s per annum.

THE RULES OF GOLF COMMITTEE

The R&A is first and foremost a private club for its members, who number in excess of 2,000 all over the world, but it is also the governing body of the game in most of the world, and it is now the case that formulating and updating the Rules of Golf is one of the most important functions performed by the club.

During the early nineteenth century, however, most golf clubs formed their own rules, and these worked perfectly well on their own home territory, but as golfers became more adventurous and more inquisitive they began exploring their neighbours' courses and testing their skills against their adversaries. The trouble was that each player played by his own club's rules, and these could and did vary to a great extent from those of their neighbours. Rules tended to provide remedies and penalties for situations which were peculiarly local, and opposing players were often at odds about which penalties were appropriate. A universal code of rules was necessary, and the golfing world looked to St Andrews for a solution, such was the reputation that had grown around this august body of golfers. The club's own rules, borrowed from the Honourable Company in Edinburgh, contained much that was essentially local, but the R&A was invited by other clubs to take over the Rules of Golf in 1897 and drew up a universal code, allowing clubs to supplement these with local rules to meet local contingencies.

The Rules of Golf Committee now comprises members of the R&A and co-opted members from golf authorities at home and overseas. The United States Golf Association retains control of rule-making in the USA and Mexico, but the two authorities meet every four years to revise the rules in the face of changing conditions. The R&A has become the ruling body of golf in all parts of the world except those covered by the United States Golf Association.

THE CHAMPIONSHIP COMMITTEE

The R&A trophy cabinet, containing the Open Championship Claret Jug, the original Championship Belt won outright by Tommy Morris in 1870, and the large Amateur Championship Trophy (Span photo)

To the average golfer, the most exciting of the R&A's duties is the organisation of the Open Championship through the Championship Committee. The Open is the oldest golf championship in the world, having been instituted by Prestwick Golf Club in 1860 to determine who was 'the champion golfer' for the year.

The Open Championship is not the most lucrative tournament, but it is certainly the most prestigious – it is the championship all golfers want to win. The name of the event tells the whole story. It is the Open Golf Championship not the British Open, as it is erroneously referred to by many people. To call it the British Open is to diminish its status from a universal to a national event.

General Dwight Eisenhower exercising his right, as an honorary member of the R&A, to play on the Old Course – but not from the first tee. The great soldier funked the ordeal of playing the first hole and took his first drive from the second

Since 1919, the club has been responsible for the organisation of the Open and also the Amateur Golf Championship. From 1872 the Open Championship was organised by the clubs on the championship rota. Originally, there were three – Prestwick Golf Club, the Honourable Company and the R&A – but by 1919 the rota had been increased to six by the addition of Royal Liverpool, Royal St George's and Deal. In that year the R&A was invited by the other clubs to take over control of the Open. The Amateur followed more or less the same pattern, with the organising clubs asking the R&A in 1919 to take over control of the championships. The Championship Committee also has responsibility for organising the British Mid Amateur Championship, the Boys Amateur Championship, Walker Cup matches when they are played in the British Isles, and the selection of teams for Great Britain and Ireland international matches.

St Andrews overtook Prestwick as the most used venue, when the 25th Open was staged over the Old Course in 1995. St Andrews has prospered as an Open Championship venue, while others, such as Prestwick and Musselburgh, have disappeared from the rota.

There was a time when it seemed the Open Championship had lost its attraction for United States players. Between the wars, and particularly during the period 1921 to 1933, Americans won all but one of the Open titles. Sam Snead renewed a fleeting United States interest by winning at St

Andrews in 1946, and he probably put his finger on the problem when he said that the prize money for the winner – £150 – was derisory.

There was a time when winning the title was all that mattered – the perks came later. A new or ambitious golf club would offer a handsome retainer, club- and ball-markers would offer financial inducements, and there were exhibition matches to be played. This was how success was measured in the 1930s. After the Second World War, money was the main factor. Henry Gullen, 'Mr Golf' as he was known throughout the world, died in 1940, having been secretary of the R&A for 28 years. Mr William Hardie, his assistant, carried on for a few years until the appointment of Commander J.A. Storar Carson in 1946. When he quit the job in 1952, prize money had risen from £1,000 to £2,450, but still the Americans seemed uninterested. One or two still came over, such as Johnny Bulla, Frank Stranahan, Ben Hogan – who won at Carnoustie in 1953 – and Ed Furgol. But they were not coming in the numbers which the Championship Committee wished.

Commander Storar Carson was followed by Brigadier Eric Brickman, who was to serve the club for the next 17 years. He was a man of great personal charm, and he literally charmed the Americans into the Open. There was, of course, the promise of gold, for the prize fund rose from £2,450 to nearly £20,000. It took a little time but he persuaded Arnold Palmer to compete in the Centenary Open in 1960. Palmer finished runner-up to Kel Nagle, but he came back in 1961 and 1962, winning the title each time. Such was Arnold Palmer's reputation in the States that where he went, other Americans followed, and so the Open Championship began again to welcome the cream of the United States players. Jack Nicklaus, Tom Watson, Tony Lema, Doug Sanders and many others became regular contenders.

When Brigadier Brickman retired he was followed by Keith Mackenzie, who accelerated and expanded his work. Mackenzie was followed by Michael Bonallack in 1983, who, in turn, was succeeded by Peter Dawson in 1999. By 2005, the Open prize fund had grown to £3,855,000, with the winner taking home £750,000.

THE LINKS FOR SALE

The decline of St Andrews as a centre of political, industrial and educational importance began in the sixteenth century with the Reformation when Catholicism was ousted by Protestantism as the established Church. Religious administration made a clean break with St Andrews and became centred elsewhere, and the town ceased to be a point of pilgrimage.

During the late eighteenth century the town's misfortunes were compounded by inept and profligate local government which allowed the town to deteriorate to such an extent that there was a real threat to transfer the university to Perth.

As the town's income decreased, the Town Council sold off part of its patrimony; but the more it sold, the less income it earned, and so things went on until the council was nearly bankrupt. Did it pull in its belt? Not a bit of it. Dr David Hay Fleming, a noted Scottish historian, writing at the turn of the century, described the council's 'endless convivialities'. 'It seems to have become impossible,' he wrote, 'to discuss even trivial municipal matters without the aid of wine and punch, and greater matters were celebrated with an abundance of strong liquor.'

Things came to a head in January 1797 when the Town Council considered a report on their finances and looked at ways of 'extricating themselves from their present difficulties'. They thought they might be able to borrow what they wanted from the magistrates on the security of what was left of the town's patrimony. This failed to materialise, but in February 1797 two merchants, Robert Gourlay and John Gunn, offered to act as trustees for the Town Council and to provide the money. Gourlay and Gunn, being hard-headed businessmen, asked for a bond over the Links as security for the loan. The amount advanced was £2,080 7s 11d, and Gourlay and Gunn had the power to sell 'whole or part of the subjects by public roup against Martinmas next' – in other words by public auction the following November. They were quick to act on this because on 30 October 1797 part of the land 'comprising the lands of Pilmor and Pilmor Links' was acquired by Thomas Erskine of Cambo for £805.

Two years later, Erskine wanted to sell the land but as the joint owner was a minor – his granddaughter – there was some difficulty in granting a valid title to the would-be purchasers, so Erskine, Gourlay and Gunn petitioned the council to grant a disposition of the land to father and son, Charles and Cathcart Dempster, and the transaction was completed on 4 December 1799.

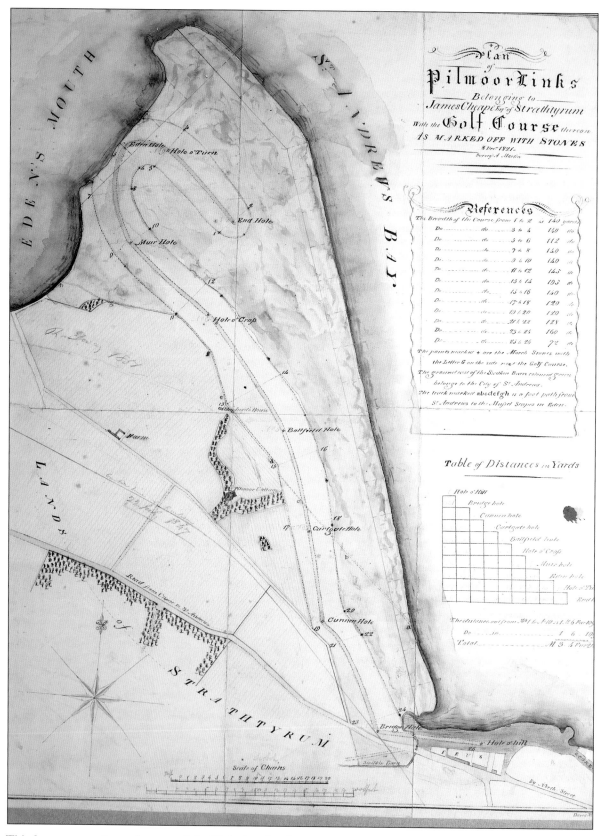

This famous map shows the area of the Links forming James Cheape's purchase in 1821, which finally put an end to the Rabbit Wars. The layout of the Old Course is clearly defined, and there is even a card of the course with the contemporary names and lengths of the holes. The total length of the course is shown as 3 miles, 4 furlongs and 218 yards – 6,378 yards – only a little less than today's length from the medal tees of 6,721 yards (reproduced by kind permission of the Royal and Ancient Golf Club of St Andrews)

The disposition contained several safeguards, one of which was 'that no hurt or damage shall be done thereby to the golf links, nor shall it be in the power of any proprietor of said Pilmor Links to plough up any part of the said golf links in all time coming but the same is reserved entirely as it has been in all times past for the comfort and amusement of the inhabitants and others who shall resort thither for that amusement'. This very important phrase was to be mirrored in the later Acts of Parliament concerning the Links.

The area concerned in the sale was 280 acres bounded by the sea and the Swilcan Burn on the east, the Water of Eden on the north, and part of the lands of Strathtyrum on the west and south. It should be noted that the portion of the Old Course now forming the first and 18th fairways and lying to the east of the Swilcan Burn was not included in the sale and has never been out of public ownership.

The Dempsters were merchants with wide-ranging interests in St Andrews, and they saw a means of further diversifying their commercial activities by introducing rabbits to the Links to provide meat and pelts. But the rabbits did what rabbits do best, and within a short time the Links, including the golfing area, was a vast rabbit warren and practically ruined as a golf course.

This was seen by local golfers and members of the Society of St Andrews Golfers to be a violation of the conditions of sale. In October 1801 Mr George Cheape, who was then captain of the society, complained to the Town Council about the destruction of the golfing area, and early in 1803 the society launched an appeal for funds so that they could fight the matter in the Court of Session. Subscriptions came to the fund from many parts of the world, including India and the West Indies. The fund reached almost £1,000, a staggering figure in those days. The council joined in and in 1806 supported the case in the Court of Session, asking that the inhabitants of St Andrews and others should be at liberty to destroy the rabbits. The joint action by the club and the Town Council was successful but the Dempsters were defiant. They appealed to the House of Lords, arguing that the golfing area formed only about ten acres of the 280 acres of the Links, and because of this they ought not to be prevented from pursuing a legitimate commercial undertaking. The Lords gave a qualified response to the appeal and suggested that the case should be taken back to the Court of Session. The Dempsters did not take advantage of this ruling, and in the meantime the Rabbit Wars continued, with the local golfers and the society members killing the rabbits and feuding violently with the Dempsters' tenants when they tried to intervene.

The conflict was ended in 1821 – not by the courts but by Mr James Cheape, Laird of Strathtyrum, who bought the feu of the Links from the Dempsters. Announcing the purchase at the annual dinner of the society in that year, Mr Cheape said, 'In doing this, I am confident that in putting an end to all future litigation, I am rendering a service to my successors as well as to the Society.' He acquired the land for an annual feu duty, or ground rent, of £42, and in 1848 his brother George, who by this time had succeeded to the estate, redeemed the feu duty.

TIMES IMPROVE

This statue of the Hindu deity Siva with his consort Parvati graces the office of the principal of St Andrews University. Strips of gutta percha were packed around the statue to protect it in transit from Malaya, where the Revd James Paterson was a missionary. Paterson sent the statue to his father with instructions to pass it on to the university. Robert Adams Paterson, James's younger brother, heated and moulded the gutta percha into the first 'gutty' golf ball in 1848 (St Andrews University)

I n Victorian times, and probably before then, the Links were used for a variety of activities. Dean of Guild W.T. Linskill, a local historian, recalls the scene as he saw it in 1874:

Wolfe-Murray could be seen riding round the Links on a white pony, I remember people washing clothes in tubs at the Swilcan Burn and bleaching clothes on the whin bushes and on the Ladies' Course [the Himalayas]. Carpet beating was common between Grannie Clark's Wynd and the Swilcan, and I have actually seen cricket and football being played there. There were all sorts of amusements and booths in the Games Hollow, erroneously now called the Bow Butts. The real Bow Butts were farther east near the foot of Butts Wynd.

Another non-golfing activity seen frequently on the Links during the 1860s was the playing of croquet by men and women in front of the R&A clubhouse.

The fortunes of golf and St Andrews took a decisive turn for the better in the mid-nineteenth century with the invention of the gutta ball. The first gutta was made in St Andrews by a schoolboy, Robert Adams Paterson. By displacing the expensive featherie ball, it brought the game within the reach of many who, until then, could not afford to play. It was not good news for the members of the R&A, for they had quite voluntarily taken it upon themselves to meet the cost of maintaining the golf course. As more people began to play golf, fewer starting times were available for the members. There was also a bigger bill for maintenance, for the indestructible gutta encouraged the development of iron-headed clubs. Every divot raised by a visiting cleek increased the cost of maintenance.

Another important factor in the improvement of St Andrews was the coming of Sir Hugh Lyon Playfair, who retired from the army in 1834, having served most of his 30 years with the artillery in India. He became provost of St Andrews in 1842 and set about cleaning up the town. He was a keen golfer and became captain of the R&A in 1856. His enthusiasm for the game of golf and his love for St Andrews were twin interests which brought great benefits to the town and to golf.

The St Andrews–Leuchars railway line, which skirted the golf courses and formed the southern boundary of the 16th fairway of the Old Course until the late 1960s, was a feature of the Links. It had its beginnings in 1845, when a survey was made with a view to the construction of a branch line to St Andrews of the Edinburgh and Northern Company's line at Guardbridge. The proposed line would have separated the green at the Burn Hole (then the first, now the 17th) from the rest of the course. The R&A naturally objected to this particular section of the line and formed a special committee to oppose it. They were successful, and the railway company agreed to modify their scheme so that the line was carried farther south so as to avoid the green. The line was opened in 1852 and closed in 1969.

As Provost Playfair's improvements took place, and the pigsties and dunghills disappeared from the streets and the air sweetened, more and more people took advantage of the new railway line to flock to St Andrews to enjoy its bracing breezes and sea-bathing and to play the national game of golf. This was of great benefit to the economy of the town, but because there was only one course and golf was free, crowding became intolerable. The reality was that another course was needed; and space for a new course had made itself available by a process of natural reclamation from the sea.

In April 1893 St Andrews Town Council formed a committee 'to consider the propriety and practicality of increasing the golfing facilities on the links'. One month later, the R&A appointed a Special Committee to confer with the proprietor of the Links, Mr Cheape, with a view to purchase. The club had told the Town Council that they would continue to maintain the course

ABOVE LEFT:
The engine continues to belch out smoke while the driver has a privileged view of play on the 16th green in one of the Amateur Championship matches of 1936. The railway link to St Andrews brought tourists to play golf and spectators to watch big matches

ABOVE RIGHT: Sir Hugh Lyon Playfair, provost of St Andrews from 1842 to 1861 and captain of the R&A in 1856, when two holes were cut on each green of the Old Course, thus inaugurating the system of double greens peculiar to St Andrews (St Andrews University)

as they had done in the past but they made it clear that they were under no obligation to do so. The club would not interfere with the public's privilege of walking over all the Links, but they refused to give written acknowledgement of that right.

The Town Council was firmly of the opinion that what the club really wanted was a course from which they could exclude others. They wrote to Mr Cheape, asking him not to enter into any bargain with any other party until they had had the opportunity of considering whether to make an offer, but Mr Cheape refused to bind himself in any way in regard to the sale of the Links.

In August 1893 the Town Council sought the opinion of Dr Thomas Thornton of Dundee about courses of action which might be pursued to acquire the Links. Dr Thornton, who had his own legal practice in Dundee, was town clerk of that city and one of Scotland's leading authorities on parliamentary procedures; indeed, before his brief for St Andrews Town Council was concluded, he had been awarded a knighthood. Dr Thornton outlined three courses of action which might be taken but recommended that the Links should be purchased under a special Act of Parliament, in which case an agreement might be entered into with the proprietor and framed in the Bill.

The 17th hole (the Road Hole) looking towards the railway sheds and the station master's house. The infamous road is on the left

One member of the Town Council suggested that they should make an offer of £5,000 based on an area of 250 acres at ten shillings per acre at 40 years purchase, but the council, with a touch of parsimony, offered £4,500. The R&A offered £5,000, and Mr Cheape sold the golf links to the club.

This put the Town Council on the spot. They decided that Dr Thornton's proposal should be put into operation, and they received the support of the inhabitants, who had been invited to a public meeting. The council estimated that the cost of purchasing the Links and the expenses of promoting a private Act would be £6,000. This would require annually:

Interest on outlay at 3½%	£210
Sinking fund for 60 years	£100
Total	£310
Less estimated rents for grazing	£80
Leaving	£230

To finance this cost would require a rate per pound of something less than 1½d.

When Mr Cheape made his bargain with the R&A, he laid down several conditions, among which were the right to dig shells from the shell pits near the mouth of the River Eden and that the proprietor of Strathtyrum Estate and his family and guests resident at Strathtyrum should have the right to play golf free of charge on any new course that might be formed. He also added a pre-emption clause that if the club ever decided to sell the Links they must first offer them to him at the price they paid for them.

The club had to find the money to pay for the Links and the construction of the new course. A total of £7,000 would be required, but the members' subscription, which stood then at £3 per annum, would not be raised. The R&A Committee proposed to leave £3,000 of the purchase price on loan with Mr Cheape; to increase club membership by 100 and charge £15 entrance money, raising £1,500; and to borrow £2,500 on the security of the clubhouse.

Early golfers, probably around 1875, preparing to play over the Old Course. The golfer about to play is teeing up one club length from the hole (St Andrews University)

The R&A wrote to the Town Council, saying that the 'club are extremely sensible of the amicable feeling which had always existed between them and the townspeople as represented by the local authority. They are most anxious that no action of theirs should in any way endanger its continuance.' The club also repeated its pledge to continue to maintain the Old Course and would offer no obstacle to the continued enjoyment of the Links ground by the people of St Andrews for the purposes of walking as before.

What the letter did not state was that the inhabitants would have the right to play golf on the new course, and so the Town Council agreed to give effect to the promotion of the Bill in Parliament seeking powers of compulsory purchase. After the R&A had completed its bargain with Mr Cheape, it issued a statement that members of golf clubs who were residents of St Andrews would be permitted to play on the new course 'subject to such rules and bye-laws as may be approved by the club'.

But the legal wheels had already been set in motion. Objections to the Bill were lodged by the R&A, by Mr Cheape, and by a small group of St Andrews residents. A battle over ownership of the Links was about to begin.

THE 1894 ACT

Before the 1894 Bill went before the Scottish Select Committee, sub-committees of the Town Council and the R&A continued a dialogue to try to resolve the differences between the two parties.

The Bill duly went before the Select Committee on 1 May 1894 and evidence was given before Sir James Kitson as chairman.

After three days, senior counsel for the Town Council reported that agreement had been reached with the club. Under the agreement, the council would take over the ownership of the Links. The club would be responsible for the management of the Links and would construct a second course at its own expense. The club had given way on its insistence on an exclusive right for its members to play on the new course: play on both courses would be free, except that on the new course, players who were neither ratepayers of St Andrews nor members of the R&A would be required to pay a 'tariff', or green fee.

The inhabitants who had petitioned against the Bill were not parties to this agreement, and evidence continued to be led on that day (4 May) on their behalf. No evidence was led by Mr Cheape, but his counsel, addressing the committee, made it clear that Mr Cheape had not abandoned his right of pre-emption.

The Select Committee accepted that an agreement had been concluded and would be incorporated into the Bill, and the Act in due course received the Royal Assent on 20 July 1894. And so it seemed that everything had been neatly parcelled up, but details of the land to be used for the new course had still to be defined.

The R&A had commissioned a civil engineer, Mr B. Hall Blyth of Edinburgh, to lay out the new course. When his proposals were examined by the Town Council, it was clear that he intended to take up almost all of the ground between the Old Course and the sea. The council took the view that this left no room for the public to exercise its right to walk over the Links. There were further discussions between the two sub-committees, with the club threatening to take the matter back to Parliament. Eventually, agreement was reached, the Town Council making a concession that any ball accidentally going outside the demarcating boundary between old and new courses might be played and would not require to be lifted. This was not incorporated into

Two flags – one the Scottish Saltire – are flown from the Grand Hotel, which was opened in 1895. A man and two women are crossing the Swilcan Burn by the wooden bridge which leads to the New Course. To the left, on the Bruce Embankment, is the granite drinking fountain provided by St Andrews Town Council and opened by Mrs W.J. Rusack, granddaughter of Tom Morris, on 22 June 1897 – the same day as the opening of the Jubilee Course. The drinking fountain was removed for the Centenary Open in 1960, but was restored to the Links in 1997 and positioned by the first tee as part of the centenary celebrations for the Jubilee Course (D.C. Thomson)

the Act but the spirit of the agreement has been faithfully maintained, and there has never been a time when a ball played from the New Course onto the Old Course – or vice versa – has been out of bounds. On its part, the club made concessions on the amount of land required for the new course.

A few points from the Notes of Evidence might be of interest. In his opening address to the Select Committee, senior counsel for the Town Council made a statement which could have been made with just as much relevance 80 years later, in 1974: 'We are trustees for the public, and seeing there has been talk about private links from which the public are to be excluded we must have the controlling voice, and the power of approving and seeing that the regulations are not of an exclusive nature or prejudicial to the existing rights of the public.'

The evidence also revealed that, while there was general agreement, sometimes even cordiality, among the golfing 'chiefs' in both camps, there existed ripples of irritation in the ranks of the local golfing 'braves'. The locals felt that some R&A members adopted a patronising and sometimes overbearing attitude towards them.

Mr John Paterson, who had earlier served six years as provost of St Andrews, gave an example of what he called 'the incompatibility of interest as between the club and the town'. He told the Select Committee that he was the owner of three houses near the clubhouse. The ground on which the houses stood was wanted for a very large hotel – the Grand Hotel. He claimed he had sold the houses for less than their market value because he felt the hotel would be in the best interests of St Andrews. There was only one objection to the granting of a licence for the hotel, and that came from the club's committee. The advocate told the magistrates that they did not want people to come to St Andrews or to have facilities granted to them.

The hotel, the striking red sandstone building which overlooks the 18th green of the Old Course, got its licence, but the incident illustrates that the aims of the two parties to this unlikely alliance were poles apart. The Town Council wanted people to come to St Andrews to boost the economy; the R&A wanted them to stay away because their presence took up starting times, and larger numbers on the course meant bigger maintenance bills. The partnership has, however, endured through mutual trust and respect.

The main provisions of the Act may be summarised as follows. The Town Council was given power to acquire the Links from the club for £5,000 with powers of compulsory purchase if necessary. The Old Course and the new course which was to be laid out would be managed by a committee, to be known as the Green Committee of St Andrews Links, consisting of five members of the R&A and two persons nominated by the Town Council. In addition to laying out a new 18-hole course, the club would also maintain a short course (known today as the Ladies' Putting Green or 'Himalayas').

The club was empowered to levy a charge against visitors using the new course during July, August and September. The Laird of Strathtyrum, his family and guests resident at Strathtyrum were to have the right of free golf – not only over the new course, as stipulated in the Agreement, but also over the Old Course and any future course to be constructed. Whether this was by design or by error is not clear – that privilege was not discussed by the Select Committee – but it was to provide a large windfall for the Cheape family almost a hundred years later.

Sheep grazing on the Links in 1897 (St Andrews University)

Old Tom Morris about to drive off the first tee of the Old Course. This photograph was taken after 1895, as the Grand Hotel dominates the skyline on the right. The fairway in the foreground appears distinctly bare of grass (George Washington Wilson Collection)

Mr Cheape had made clear at the Select Committee hearing that he was not prepared to give up his right of pre-emption, and the dispute between Mr Cheape and the Town Council rumbled on. Nevertheless, while the arguing continued, so too did work on the new course, although the council could not get a valid title to the land until the question of pre-emption was settled. Mr Cheape had set a price of nearly £11,500 on his pre-emption, more than twice the amount he had already received for the sale of the land. After lengthy negotiations, however, he accepted the Town Council's offer of £1,500 in full settlement of the right of pre-emption, and the feu disposition between the R&A and the Town Council was signed on 15 May 1896 – more than a year after the New Course, as it was now officially called, had opened for play.

THE 1913 ACT

With the passing of the 1894 Act, the remarkable statutory partnership between the R&A and the town of St Andrews had been launched.

But all was not 'long drives and short putts' for the partners. The Act was flawed in several respects. It was a mistake to levy charges for visitors playing on the New Course during the busy summer months while golf was available free to everybody on the Old Course. Not surprisingly, this meant that golfers flocked to the Old. Neither the club nor the council had thought of incorporating in the Act provision for reserved starting times for club members and local residents, and the result was that they were almost crowded off the course by visitors during the best playing months.

Although local golfers were unhappy, the Town Council was delighted at the benefits which accrued to the economy from the increase in the number of holidaymakers. The club members had no such consolation, and within a few years the two bodies were almost at loggerheads. The situation was compounded by a series of dry, hot summers culminating in a particularly arid period in 1911, and in the early spring of 1912 cold winds swept in from the east and north, inhibiting growth on the fairways and greens. The condition of the courses was such that visitors who had come to play golf left disillusioned about the famous Old Course, which had, by that time, come to be acknowledged as the best in the world.

Complaints kept rolling in to the Town Council and the club. The two bodies formed committees which met independently and then jointly. They pinpointed the problem: congestion; and the solution: a tariff on the Old Course and the construction of a 'fourth course' of good quality. A third course, the Jubilee, had already been laid out by the Town Council, but it was of poor quality and intended only for beginners.

In the meantime, a crisis seemed to be developing in the R&A. Some members, it was rumoured, were to propose that the 1894 agreement should be abandoned and the club moved elsewhere.

Mr Horace Hutchinson, a club member and a golfer and writer of great skill, wrote that an influential section of members was to propose to the club's General Meeting that the Town Council should give up to the club the sole use of the New Course for an annual rent, and if the offer was not accepted the club should sever its connection with the courses on which the Town Council had rights and move to some other ground where it would have a free hand. Mr Hutchinson did not suggest explicitly that the club should remove from St Andrews but there was an implicit threat.

The editor of *The Sportsman* believed the threat was real. He wrote that the danger came from English members of the club 'who would no doubt like to see the Headquarters of Golf removed to London'. He was concerned for the image of the club. If it were to leave the historic headquarters of golf, its role as legislator of the game might be taken from it.

Whether or not the club's officials had 'behind-the-scenes' talks with the recusants, the sabre-rattling stopped. A report from the two 'congestion' committees went before the General Meeting and was adopted with only minor amendments.

Under the agreement, starting times on the Old Course between 10 a.m. and 11.16 a.m. and 2 p.m. and 3.16 p.m. would be reserved for R&A members, and starting times on the Old Course would be made available for local golfers on Thursday and Saturday afternoons. The receipts from the Old Course, the Jubilee Course and the proposed fourth course would belong to the Town Council; those from the New Course would belong to the club.

The Town Council was empowered to levy charges for play on the Old Course but not against municipal voters, members of the R&A or members of the Cheape family and guests. The Town Council could reduce charges for various classes of golfer such as university students and members of local golf clubs who were not permanently resident in St Andrews. The management of the Jubilee Course and the fourth course would be in the hands of a committee comprising five members nominated by the Town Council and two nominated by the R&A. The Cheape family and their guests at Strathtyrum had rights to six starting times per day – three in the morning and three in the afternoon. These could be taken all on one course or spread over all four.

These agreed arrangements could not be implemented without a further provisional order amending the 1894 Act. The Town Council held a plebiscite of the local electorate, who voted 1,159 in favour and 160 against promoting the order. The 1913 Act passed through Parliament without opposition and received the Royal Assent on 10 July 1913.

The new regulations giving concession rates to members of local golf clubs not permanently resident in the town proved to be a boon to the clubs, for many people all over the country recognised this as an inexpensive way to spend a golfing holiday in St Andrews. The St Andrews Golf Club and the New Golf Club found their 'country membership' growing so quickly that it almost outnumbered the local membership. The new Act seemed to work out well for all parties because the Business Meeting of the R&A in May 1914 was told that the club membership had rocketed to 1,026 – the highest it had ever been.

It might be useful at this point to reflect upon how the R&A had fared during the period between the two Acts. Their maintenance costs over the years had been:

1896 – £613	1906 – £830	1907 – £814
1908 – £951	1909 – £893	1910 – £897
1911 – £1,234	1912 – £2,241 (estimated)	

The percentage of starting times enjoyed by the club members in the peak holiday periods in 1911 and 1912 were:

1911 – July 13%	August 22%
1912 – July 8%	August 19%

It will be seen that the members had a grievance, for while their costs had risen, their access to the courses had diminished. But it was not one-sided, for local golfers experienced the same frustration in seeking starting times.

One of the obligations placed upon the Town Council by the new Act was the provision of a fourth course. There were two possible solutions: the reclamation of more land from the sea; or the acquisition of ground on the landward side of the Old Course. The first would be a time-consuming process, and the course was needed urgently. The other alternative was more appealing. The Town Council already owned some land lying south of the 12th fairway of the Old Course but it was densely colonised by whin bushes. The remainder belonged to James Cheape of Strathtyrum – the same James Cheape who had sold the Links to the R&A. The Town Council opened negotiations with him for a lease of two fields south of the railway which were tenanted as playing fields by Madras College and Clifton Bank School, and three fields lying between the railway line and the Old Course. Mr Cheape was very co-operative, and a 25-year lease was negotiated beginning at Martinmas (November) 1913 at an annual rental of £130. The fourth course was laid out by H.S. Colt of Sunningdale and opened as the Eden Course on 4 July 1914.

THE 1924 ACT

An old print of the first and 18th fairways of the Old Course, showing, on the right, the old Swilcan Bridge and the Lifeboat House, which figured in a deal between the Town Council and the R&A over an extension to the R&A Clubhouse. Skirting the right-hand side of the fairway is the line of the Links Road, scene of the 'war' in 1880. At the upper end of the road is Hugh Philp's shop and Allan Robertson's house, and to the left is the old Union Parlour (St Andrews University)

The 1913 Act seemed to have solved the problems which bedevilled the early days of the Town–R&A partnership, and there was no further legislation until 1924, when the R&A wished to make a small addition to the clubhouse. For this they needed 30 square yards of land at the north-east corner of the building, and the Town Council was willing to sell. So where did the problem lie?

The Town Council had forgotten the lessons of the 1894 Act – that they could not dispose of any of the Links land without parliamentary authority. They believed all they had to do in the disposal of any municipal property was to advertise it for sale by roup. It was left to a St Andrean living in Edinburgh, David Balsillie, to jog the council's memory. He reminded the council of the need for parliamentary sanction and added that he was concerned not so much with the need to cede ground to the club but with the principle involved – 'for if the Corporation can presume to expropriate any fraction of the links in the fashion indicated the proposition naturally arises: how much more public territory might not be similarly alienated?'

The Town Council did follow the proper procedure and petitioned Parliament for a new order, which passed through the legislature and received the Royal Assent on 29 May 1924. And what was the effect of the 1924 Act? The Town Council was empowered to feu 30 square yards of the Links to the R&A for a feu duty of five shillings (25 pence) per annum.

THE 1932 ACT

The principal effect of this Act was to enable gate money to be charged for admission to major golf events played over St Andrews Links. It represented a violent break with tradition, for the public had had the right from time immemorial to walk freely and unhindered over the Links.

Some mechanism had to be found to control the crowds which invaded championship courses all over the country whenever a major event was staged. It was a healthy sign for the game, but Prestwick had borne the brunt of spectator indiscipline in 1925. As a result, a charge was imposed for spectating at the Amateur Championship at Muirfield and the Open Championship at Lytham in 1926. Money proved to be an effective regulating device. St Andrews was different from other championship venues in that the public had a statutory right to walk over the courses. However, the conduct of the crowds at the finals of the British Ladies Championship in 1929 and the Amateur Championship in 1930 convinced the R&A Championship Committee that a solution must be found.

When the Championship Committee in 1931 was considering possible venues for the 1933 Open Championship, it was clear that the claims of St Andrews had been prejudiced by the events of 1929 and 1930. The committee told the Town Council that St Andrews might get the Open if crowds were regulated by the charging of gate money which would become the property of the committee. By pure coincidence, the provost of St Andrews at that time was W. Norman Boase who was also chairman of the R&A's Championship Committee.

When the council seemed to be dragging its feet, not so much over the charging of gate money but as to who was to get it, Provost Boase took a hard line, telling the council, 'Either you want the championship or you don't.'

The councillors were unwilling to risk losing the Open, and they agreed to the proposals. They managed, however, to extract this promise from the Championship Committee: 'Not one penny will go to the R&A Golf Club. The charges will be made not with the object of making a profit but to regulate play.' The Provisional Order went through unopposed, receiving the Royal Assent on 16 June 1932. The maximum charge per day was fixed at five shillings (25 pence), and the Town Council was given power to exempt any person or class of person from the charges.

THE 1946 ACT

The Links Act of 1946 was probably the most important of all the Links Acts, apart from the first in 1894, for it removed from the people of St Andrews the right to free golf over the Links – a right which they had enjoyed for as long as golf had been played.

The removal of this ancient right, drastic though it may have appeared to St Andreans, was a measure of the respect and goodwill which had been generated over the years between the townspeople of St Andrews and the members of the Royal and Ancient Golf Club. The truth is that the R&A was in deep financial trouble and had to admit that it was unable to meet its commitments under the 1894 Act to maintain the Old and New courses. The partnership between the town and the club was about to be put to the test.

A costly war had just been concluded, and the club found the expense of maintaining the courses was becoming prohibitive because of the ever-increasing cost of labour and machinery. The club bravely offered to maintain the courses in good condition 'even at the expense of the members', but had to add 'there is, of course, a limit to what can be undertaken by a club of about 800 members'.

The club claimed it cost £3,000 a year to maintain the courses before the war and estimated that they could not now be maintained for less than £4,500. The suggestion was made that the Town Council might help by making a contribution of £1,500 a year and that this could be raised by making a charge against local golfers.

The Town Council agreed to promote a provisional order seeking power to charge local people for golf, and to make a contribution to the club. They did not, however, commit themselves to the extent of help which might be given.

The townspeople had not been consulted about the proposed measure and asked for a public meeting to be held. The request was turned down by the council. The torch for the local people was taken up by St Andrews Golf Club, whose membership covered a wide cross-section of the St Andrews community. The St Andrews Golf Club fought a hard and unyielding battle with the Town Council and gave notice that they were not prepared to give the council 'a blank cheque' to charge what they wanted. It was then that Provost George Bruce gave an undertaking that the clubs in St Andrews would be consulted before any charges were levied and that the rates charged against local people would not exceed 25 per cent of those charged against other classes of golfer.

The St Andrews Golf Club was mollified; it had not got everything it wanted, but it had demonstrated to the Town Council that the council's role in such matters was to serve the people and not to direct them.

It seemed the way was clear for the Town Council to proceed to Parliament, but the Secretary of State for Scotland appointed a tribunal to hear evidence in the case in Edinburgh. It appeared that five weeks after the date for lodging objections a petition had been delivered to the Secretary of State and that three of the petitioners wished to speak against the order.

The petitioners did not, however, have the benefit of legal representation, and Mr J.L. Clyde, KC, the Town Council's senior counsel, was therefore placed in the unusual position of having to put up among his own witnesses people who were going to attack the provisions of the order. This looked rather like an audacious, even defiant, act by the petitioners, but it was capped afterwards by one of the petitioners who claimed £8 1s 8d (about £8.08) from the Town Council as expenses for attending the tribunal – and she got it.

The tribunal produced few fireworks but there were one or two points which are worthy of note. Mr Clyde, in his opening address, gave an assurance that members of the R&A who lived in St Andrews would lose the privilege of free golf and would be on the same level as other people who lived in the town. When he referred to the privilege of free golf enjoyed by the Laird of Strathtyrum he said, 'The proprietor of Strathtyrum never himself played golf, his successors never have played golf but we felt that if the provision was in, there was no great harm, particularly if they did not play golf.' It was also revealed in evidence that the annual subscription paid by members of the R&A was £6 and that it had remained unchanged for 25 years. With the tribunal completed, the order passed through Parliament and became law on 19 December 1946.

The main provisions were that the Town Council was empowered to make contributions to the R&A for the maintenance of the Old and New courses, provided that the club had spent at least £4,000 on these courses in the preceding year. No minimum or maximum contribution was specified. The council was given power to levy charges for golf against local people but with an upper limit of £2 per year. A big disappointment for locals was that the limitation of the charge against them to no more than 25 per cent of that charged against other classes of golfer was not written into the Act. But the Town Council honoured the promise made by Provost Bruce in every increase of charge until the passing of the 1974 Act.

On the other hand, while it was quite explicit in the evidence given before the tribunal that R&A members who lived in St Andrews would pay the same charges as other local people, this was not written into the Act. For a year or two, green fees were paid, but in 1952 it was reported than an R&A member who lived locally had been playing golf without paying green fees. The council considered that the practice of charging R&A members was 'based on a mistaken interpretation of the Act' and should be discontinued.

OVERLEAF: The Links peninsula with all 99 holes, the West Sands and the Eden Estuary (Peter Boardman)

THE 1953 AGREEMENT

The 1946 Act did not seem to be working well. The townspeople had lost their right to free golf but the Act had done little to cure the ills of the R&A. The club had hoped for an annual contribution of £1,500 from the Town Council but in the years from 1946 to 1950 they had received only £500 a year, with an increase in 1951 and 1952 to £750. Was the Town Council being just a little parsimonious in its help to the club? One thing was clear: neither party was happy with the arrangement.

In late 1952 a joint finance sub-committee of the club and the council had a series of meetings, during which the sub-committee had reached agreement on the principle of joint management of the courses. However, the club had refused to accept the sub-committee's recommendations.

After hearing all this at its meeting in January 1953, the Town Council made an immediate and pointed response. The council felt it had been generous in offering the club an equal partnership in the management of the Links, and left the club in no doubt that if it declined the offer there would be no partnership at all.

The club accepted the offer and both sides got together to work out details of the new partnership. The basis of the agreement was to combine the management of the courses in the interests of efficiency and economy. The Green Committee of St Andrews Links, which looked after the Old and New courses, and the Town Links Committee, which looked after the Eden and Jubilee courses, were to be combined to form a Joint Links Committee. All four courses would thus be managed by a single committee comprising five members appointed by the R&A and five nominated by the Town Council. The chairman would be one of the R&A appointees. All machinery and stock would come under the control of the Joint Committee, as would the greenkeeping staffs. The town clerk would be secretary, and no substantial change in existing policy and practice would be made without the approval of the Town Council and the club.

The financial arrangements were complicated, but financial corners were cut and both sides agreed that the annual deficit on the four courses would be shared equally by the council and the club. This meant that the running of the courses was geared to ensure an annual loss. If the courses were to show a profit, it would mean that while the locals had lost their right to free golf, R&A members were contributing nothing. That would have destroyed the equity on which trust between R&A members and townspeople had been based.

Some members of the Town Council and many of the townspeople had misgivings about the new proposals, claiming that no agreement could overturn an Act of Parliament. There may have been a haunting suspicion of this in the mind of the council as a whole, for the new agreement was to stand for a trial period of three years from 15 May 1953. In fact, it was to endure for 20 years.

One St Andrews citizen, Mr Edward P. Kyle, felt so strongly about the 1953 Agreement that in 1965 he took the opinion of counsel, who advised:

> The Memorialist might well succeed in court, but the net result of his efforts would be so small having regard to the expense involved that I would recommend him not to raise an action. It should be remembered that any action which was raised would probably be fought hard by the Town Council; the action would be very complex and consequently very expensive to lose at any point.

Mr Kyle allowed the matter to rest.

The Town Council reviewed the situation in 1963 and decided there was no need for change, and the agreement continued for the rest of the Town Council's life.

OLD COURS

Length of Holes on the Old Course

Hole No	Name	Yards	Hole No	Name	Yards
1	Burn	368	10	Tenth	312
2	Dyke	401	11	High coming home	164
3	Cartgate going out	356	12	Heathery coming home	314
4	Ginger Beer	427	13	Hole o'Cross coming home	410
5	Hole o'Cross going out	530	14	Long	527
6	Heathery going out	367	15	Cartgate coming home	409
7	High going out	352	16	Corner of the Dyke	348
8	Short	150	17	Road	467
9	End	306	18	Tom Morris	364

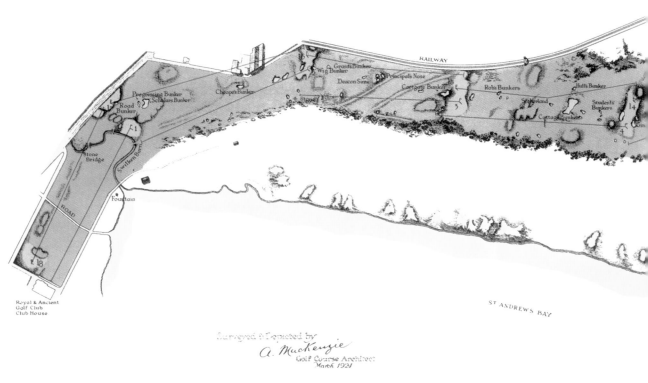

Surveyed & Depicted by
A. MacKenzie
Golf Course Architect
March 1924

ST. ANDREWS

This splendidly detailed 1924 map shows the Old Course much as it is today, with double greens, the
R&A Clubhouse, the railway line (now disused), and the driving line at the 17th hole over the famous
black sheds (reproduced by kind permission of the Royal and Ancient Golf Club of St Andrews)

THE 1967 ACT

The famous road running hard behind the green at the 17th hole of the Old Course. The Road Hole bunker is just to the left of the green, increasing the danger awaiting a less than perfectly struck approach shot. At the time of the 1946 Open, the road had not been surfaced with tarmac (D.C. Thomson)

The 1967 Links Act was a short one which abolished the limit on charges for spectators imposed in the 1932 and 1946 Links Acts. It also gave the Town Council a free hand to close the other courses while major golfing events were being played over the Old Course. It came about because the Aluminium Company of Canada wanted to inaugurate the ALCAN Tournament at St Andrews from 5 to 8 October 1967, and they asked that power be sought to increase the admission charges. Shortly afterwards, the R&A Championship Committee asked that restrictions on the charges should be removed. The committee's request was, in fact, imperative; it was to be a condition of all future championships coming to St Andrews. The Championship Committee had come a long way since 1932, when their chairman gave the assurance that gate money was purely a device for regulating the crowds. It had now become an important financial factor in the Championship Committee's plans. The Act received the Royal Assent on 14 July 1967.

THE 1974 ACT

The 1974 Links Act authorised the Town Council to hand over control and management of the courses to St Andrews Links Trust and Management Committee which were set up by the Act. The Act was necessary to allay concern that control and management of the Links would, under the provisions of local government reform, fall into the hands of some distant local authority, out of touch with the great golfing heritage and traditions which had grown around the famous Links. The Links were common ground and therefore the property of the local authority holding jurisdiction over it.

When, in 1969, Lord Wheatley published a report recommending changes in local government in Scotland, it was clear that town councils and county councils would be abolished and replaced by more broadly based district councils and regional councils. No hard and fast boundaries were defined in the report but tentative proposals indicated that Fife as an administrative authority would disappear, with one part coming under the control of Angus – or Tayside as it came to be known – and the southern portion forming part of Lothian.

It was agonisingly clear to the people of St Andrews that control of the historic golf links would be taken from them and placed with some far-off parks department either in Dundee or Edinburgh.

As things turned out, Fife county councillors and others fought and won a hard battle to keep their identity, and Fife was retained as a region, divided into three districts – Dunfermline, Kirkcaldy and North East Fife. St Andrews fell within the boundaries of the last named, whose administrative centre was to be at Cupar, only ten miles from St Andrews. It was certainly a better outcome than local people had expected. While the 'Fight for Fife' was going on, the people of St Andrews – with the power and influence of the Royal and Ancient Golf Club behind them – had fought to hold onto the Links.

The Town Council had seemed curiously reluctant to resist the Wheatley recommendations, and there was a sense of inevitability in a minute of a meeting of the council's General Purposes Committee of 8 June 1970 which stated: 'It was agreed that nothing could be gained by attempting to prevent the Town Council's ownership of the links or their share in the management and control of the golf courses passing to another authority in the event of reorganisation of local government.'

In the meantime, the R&A and the New Golf Club had been thinking along parallel lines – that control and management of the golf courses should be vested in a local consortium or trust. Several meetings were held with other local golf clubs under the auspices of the R&A, and eventually a meeting was arranged with the Town Council. Shortly after the meeting, the R&A issued a statement dated 27 May 1971. The club suggested that the Town Council should act at once to amend or repeal the Links Acts with a view to vesting control of all the courses in an independent Links trust. They also suggested the formation of a management committee to carry out the work previously performed by the Joint Links Committee. The Town Council agreed to proceed with a petition to Parliament for the formation of a St Andrews Links Trust and a St Andrews Links Management Committee. The Trust was to consist of three persons nominated by the local authority (North East Fife District Council), three nominated by the R&A, one nominated by the Secretary of State for Scotland, and the Member of Parliament for the constituency. The Trust was to appoint its own chairman annually.

The Management Committee would comprise four persons nominated by the local authority and four nominated by the R&A. It would have power to appoint its own chairman, who would not have a casting vote. In the event of opinions being evenly divided, the matter would be referred to the Trust for resolution.

The R&A had favoured the appointment of nominees from local golf clubs on the Management Committee but the Town Council demurred. They pointed out that the local authority could appoint nominees from the clubs if they so desired, and as an act of faith and precedent the Town

Council appointed William Robertson, captain of St Andrew Golf Club, and Ian Joy, a past captain of the New Golf Club, to membership of the first Management Committee set up after the passing of the Act.

A request was made that the charges to be levied against local golfers should be restricted to 25 per cent of the charges levied against others, as promised in 1946 by Provost Bruce. The R&A objected, and the Town Council compromised by restricting the amount to one third of the ordinary charge. The club was still unhappy, and so the Town Council agreed that the limitation could be altered if an application was made to the Secretary of State for Scotland. This seriously diluted the statutory protection which local people were expecting from the new Act.

The main difference between 1953 and 1974 was that the Town Council, as the 'higher court' with powers of veto over the decisions of the Joint Links Committee, was democratically elected by the residents, while from 1974 onwards they had little say in the appointment of members to the Links Trust or the Management Committee.

How had the local people fared since 1894? They had lost the right to free golf under the 1946 Act, and since 1974 their concession-rate green fee had been increased from a quarter to a third, and even this could be removed by the Secretary of State for Scotland without the need for parliamentary approval. The right to concession spectator rates granted in the 1932 and 1946 Acts had been removed by the 1967 Act. The only concession which had remained was the right to alternate starting times on the Old Course on Thursday and Saturday afternoons.

How had the various Acts affected the position of the R&A? They had been relieved of the obligation to maintain the Old and New courses; the club members were entitled to free golf on all the courses in return for the payment by the club to the Links Trust of an annual lump sum, but the 1974 Act laid down no formula for the calculation of this 'lump sum' and it has been determined largely on the basis of goodwill between the Trust and the club. The members had also gained a statutory right in the 1974 Act, subject to certain limitations, of every alternate starting time on the New Course.

An important clause in the 1974 Act gave the Trustees power to lease part of the Links and to acquire land for the purpose of improving and extending facilities for golf. While control and management of the Links was vested in the Links Trust and the Management Committee, ownership of the Links remained with the local authority. This raises the question of who owns land acquired or to be acquired by the Trust after 1974. The Act is not explicit about this, and if the time ever comes that the Trust is to be disbanded or substantially altered in its constitution or function, the question of ownership might have to be decided by the courts.

Golfers search for a ball while a walker exercises his rights (Masakuni Akiyama)

No further Acts were promulgated between 1974 and 2008, but the 1974 Act, which was due to fall in 1984, was 'continued' indefinitely by the Secretary of State for Scotland following an application by North East Fife District Council, the relevant local authority at the time. It was not long, however, before the 'indefinite continuation' was to be challenged.

Only 12 years later, in 1996, following a further revision of local government structures in Scotland, North East Fife District Council was replaced as the owner of the Links by the much larger, and more distant, Fife Council.

This was, in effect, the transference of ownership of the renowned Links from East Fife to West Fife. There had always been differences – cultural and political – between the eastern and western parts of the county: the east was dependent mainly on farming and fishing, the west on coal mining; and these differences burgeoned into suspicions which revealed themselves in 1998 when it was confirmed that Fife Council was considering a review of the 1974 Links Act. The Act was due, as were all local Acts, to lapse after 31 December 1999 unless the Secretary of State for Scotland decided otherwise, and in 1996 the Secretary of State had decided to exempt the 1974 Act from this provision, despite the reluctance of Fife Council to support such a move. His action did have the support of the District Council, Scottish Tourist Board, Royal and Ancient Golf Club, St Andrews Community Council, St Andrews University and many other local institutions. Fife Council, however, urged caution over taking a 'premature decision' regarding the Links and suggested a delay to enable them to review the law and to allow wide public consultation before deciding on a new management structure for the twenty-first century.

Many St Andrews people were apprehensive about the new council's motives. Some felt it was a move to take over 'a good money-spinner' and this fear was fired by one question in the council's Consultative Paper, which it still issued to the public in 1998, asking whether surpluses other than those required for golfing purposes should be credited to the St Andrews Common Good Fund – a fund controlled by Fife Council. There was another question which asked whether members of the Links Trust and Management Committee should be paid 'reasonable out-of-pocket expenses' for attendance at Trust and Committee meetings. Members of the Trust and Committee were already able to claim expenses – although few of them did. Some people took the view that this was a euphemism for authorising payment for attending meetings.

After all representations had been considered, Fife Council decided that the effectiveness of the management of the Links had been confirmed and that there was no need to change the existing arrangements. It also decided to continue the District Council's practice of nominating members of local golf clubs to the Links Management Committee and the Trustees, and the R&A did likewise. The people of St Andrews had won another important – if less dramatic – fight to retain control of the Links.

The local golfers' access to the courses has had to be increasingly protected by the Trust as pressure on the courses has increased as a result of the town's population explosion and a rise in visitor demand due to the worldwide growth in interest in the game. They were given priority in the Old Course ballot for an hour every morning and, in summer, every evening. In addition, blocks of starting times on the Jubilee, New, Strathtyrum and Castle courses were also reserved for them.

Although there had been no new legislation specific to the Links since 1974, there was legislation which had an impact on how the Links were run. This came in the form of the Charities and Trustee (Scotland) Act 2005.

The Links Trust is an independent trust, but with charitable status, and as such it fell within the scope of the new legislation, which set up the Office of the Scottish Charities Regulator (OSCR). This new body now oversaw some aspects of the administration of the Links, particularly the financial and legal ones. The result was more complex reporting requirements, but no perceivable benefit to golfers of other users of the Links.

Interestingly, Provost Bruce's promise to the townspeople in 1946 that the resident green fee would not exceed one quarter of that charged to 'others' (that is, visitors) was fulfilled again at the start of the twenty-first century, when Trustees set the prices for 2001. This was despite being allowed, under the 1974 Act, to charge up to one third of the visitor price.

ABOVE: Nearly home

OVERLEAF: The 18th green of the Old Course in summer

III

THE LINKS

PHYSICAL CHANGES
ON THE LINKS

THE OLD COURSE

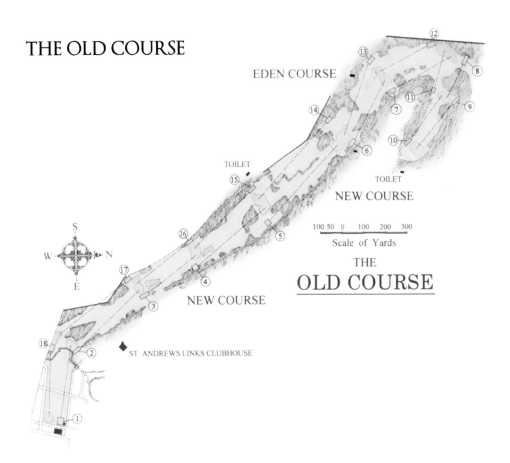

There are some who would claim that because St Andrews was the pre-Reformation ecclesiastical capital of Scotland and because charters granted by the Church played such an important part in settling the golfing patrimony on the town, there was some divine guidance in determining the path which the golf course should follow, and indeed a glance at any of the early plans of the Old Course will show that it takes the form of a crozier or bishop's pastoral crook. It follows a fairly straight path from the first tee to the sixth green, then it swings round from the dog-legged seventh and down to the eighth and ninth to form the head of the crook. From there it follows almost the same route home.

LEFT: Old Daw Anderson dispensing refreshment at the Ginger Beer Hole
to Tom Morris and his partner

Chipping over
the Swilcan Burn
(Masakuni Akiyama)

The area originally occupied by the Old Course was a very small portion of the Links – a narrow strip or cutting through the whins, formed by nature and moulded and shaped to their own needs by dedicated golfers. The word 'links' derives from the Old English 'hlinc', meaning a ridge, a baulk of land left unploughed. The reason it was left unploughed was that it was poor in plant nutrients, unfit for cultivation and of commercial use only as pasture for sheep, which can find sustenance in the shorter grasses. The Links was probably regarded by most people as wasteland.

Flocks of sheep and colonies of rabbits helped to keep the grasses short and to create narrow passages of greensward which were widened by shepherds and trappers and later by European traders transporting their merchandise from the port of St Andrews to the town markets, and finally by dedicated golfers.

In the early days of golf at St Andrews, the same holes were used for outward and inward play. The number of holes varied from time to time, but usually 11 holes were played outward and the same 11 played homeward, making a total of 22 holes. The standard round was stabilised at 18 holes in 1764. A minute of the Society of St Andrews Golfers relates that this was effected by telescoping the first four holes into two, making nine outward and nine inward. The minute reads:

> The captain and gentlemen golfers are of the opinion that it would be for the improvement of the links that the first four holes should be converted into two. They have therefore agreed that for the future they shall be played as two holes in the same way as presently marked out.

Until then, the starting point on the course seems to have been nomadic. Some historians claim that the early golfers started play on the greensward which lies to the east of the R&A Clubhouse and is now dominated by the 45-feet high obelisk of the Martyrs' Monument, familiar to millions of people who have watched golf at St Andrews on television.

There were no properly formed streets leading to the Links in those very early days, and most people, including university staff and students, went to the Links by way of Butts Wynd and then westwards along the Scores to the golfing area. Butts Wynd begins underneath the university's St Salvator's Tower, one of the dominant features of the St Andrews skyline as seen from the Links. It was so called because it led to the archery butts where young men practised – or were supposed to practise – the martial arts.

The early golfers must have been a hardy breed, for they had to fight their way through rough, rooty, heathery fairways and putt over uncut greens which sprouted more heather than grass. And it was a frustrating business if two matches going in opposite directions should meet at a green at the same time, for there was only one hole on each green and it was used by both outgoing and incoming matches.

But change was on the way. Old Daw Anderson had planted an important seed in the minds of the course's keepers when he cut two holes on the fifth green – one for the outgoing players and the other for those homeward bound. The question cropped up from time to time that it might be a good thing to have two holes cut on other greens where necessary in order to speed up play. Indeed, the historian J.B. Salmond wrote that in 1832 a proposal was put to the Society of Golfers that two holes should be cut on every green. However, he did not tell whether the proposal was approved – or, if it was, whether it was a permanent arrangement. What can be verified is that the *Fifeshire Journal*, reporting on the May meeting of the R&A in 1857, hailed the 'innovation' of double putting greens as a great success:

The second green on the Old Course

These golfers were probably playing the Old Course on the left-hand circuit (backwards on today's layout), as they appear to be driving up the 18th fairway from what is now the second tee. The year would be between 1890 and 1895 (George Washington Wilson Collection)

One hundred and twenty years later, the same scene but without anyone in range

The putting greens have had a thorough overhaul, re-turfed and otherwise improved. On each green, with the exception of the first and return, two holes have been placed; the one is played to by parties going outwards, the other in the in-coming. To prevent mistakes, the outgoing hole is supplied with a white flag, and its neighbour sports a red one, that being the colour for all the return holes. This is a decided improvement on the old system, preventing confusion and the delays which often had to be put up with, on medal days especially when a party going out encountered another winding their way homewards on the same green, there being only a hole betwixt them.

Tom Morris was keeper of the green at Prestwick at this time, so he could have no part in the origins of the double green. He was, however, closely involved in the subsequent development of the Old Course – widening the fairways and the strategic planning of the new layout.

The concept of double greens was probably the brainchild of Sir Hugh Lyon Playfair, who, as provost of St Andrews from 1842 to 1861, rejuvenated the town and hauled it out of the economic squalor in which it had wallowed since the Reformation. He was elected captain of the R&A at the autumn meeting of 1856 and was still captain during the spring meeting of 1857 when the innovation of double putting greens was introduced. Ten years earlier, he had carried out land reclamation at what we know today as the first and 18th fairways of the Old Course. At periods of high tide, the sea would encroach onto the course, causing considerable erosion. He made the reclamation by building three breakwaters across the area and infilling the spaces between them with the town refuse and covering it with soil and sand.

When Tom Morris returned to St Andrews and took over as custodian of the Links, he found that Playfair's land reclamation opened up the course for the formation of a new green on the west side of Swilcan Burn, which golfers know today as the first green. (In 1870, when the green was ready for play, it was to be the 17th.)

While Tom Morris was carrying out his returfing of the first and 18th fairways and creating the new green by the Swilcan, important work was being carried out on the approaches to the course. Links Road, which forms the boundary of the 18th fairway, was levelled off, and the path in front of the newly built R&A Clubhouse was extended to join up with Links Road. The slopes of 'The Terrace' were turfed over and a protective fence was erected. A new eighteenth green was laid out, doubling its former area.

With the introduction of the new green just to the west of the Swilcan, golfers realised that it was possible to play the course either on the original left-hand circuit or on a right-hand circuit, and for some years the course was played on the left- and right-hand circuits in alternate weeks. The right-hand circuit was preferred, for it cut out the 'crossing' at the first and 18th holes, and that circuit became the established round for the Old Course.

One effect of the change to the right-hand circuit was that many of the original bunkers are now 'blind'. This is particularly the case at the 12th, where the fairway, though peppered with bunkers, looks perfectly harmless from the tee.

During the years following the Second World War, the left-hand circuit was used occasionally during the winter months to protect the turf, but it was realised this was unfair to off-season visitors who wanted to play the championship course, and the practice was stopped in 1979.

Following a number of requests over the years from golfing journalists and curious visiting golfers, and the awareness that a new generation of St Andrews golfers had never played the course in reverse, the idea of playing the left-hand circuit again was considered by the Links Management Committee. It was decided to try it out, for historical interest, for one day only, and the day chosen was Saturday, 1 April 2000. It proved so popular that it was continued, becoming a regular event, and the number of 'reverse' days was extended to three, usually taking place around a weekend at the beginning of April.

These golfers appear to be playing the right-hand circuit of the Old Course, teeing up just to the left of the Road Hole Bunker to play the 18th (George Washington Wilson Collection)

THE NEW COURSE

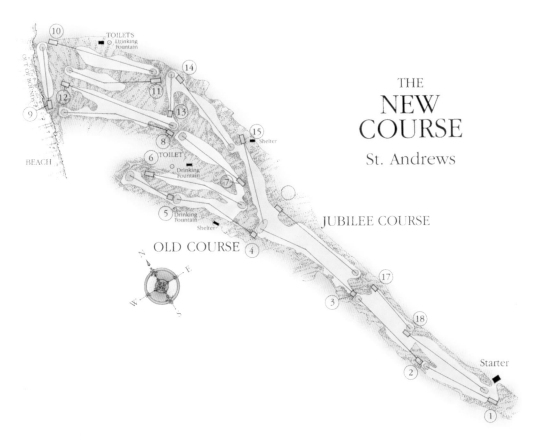

THE
**NEW
COURSE**
St. Andrews

With the passing of the 1894 Act of Parliament, the Royal and Ancient Golf Club roared into action to provide the second or New Course, although the ground did not actually come into the possession of the Town Council for another two years. The delay had been caused by the failure of the Town Council and Mr James Cheape to agree a settlement of the pre-emption in the disposition of the Links to the R&A.

The layout was planned by Mr B. Hall Blyth, a civil engineer in Edinburgh, who had negotiated the boundaries of the New Course with the Town Council. The ground supervision was entrusted to Mr R.A. Duff, of Edinburgh, who received the expert and wholehearted support of Tom Morris and his henchman, David Honeyman.

One noteworthy operation which had to be undertaken during the construction of the course was the removal of the local Volunteer Corps rifle-ranges from the landward to the seaward side of the sand dunes. The ranges remained there during the early years of the Jubilee Course, and special arrangements had to be made when shooting was in progress.

Despite the large bunker, the opening hole of the New Course is relatively benign

The New Course 10th green at sunset

70

The original layout, with only minor adjustments, endured for the next hundred years. One of the more important of these adjustments was at the 15th, which was lengthened to 394 yards, having originally been laid out as a longish short hole of 280 yards. Basically, however, the course has remained unchanged – even unspecified boundaries with the Old and Jubilee courses have remained the same. Its total original length was 6,440 yards or, as it was measured in 1895, three miles and 1,160 yards. It is now 6,362 yards from the tees for normal play, and 6,625 yards from the medal trees.

The course was opened for play on 10 April 1895 but there is no evidence of a formal opening ceremony. Perhaps the closest one can get to a formal opening was the playing of the first professional tournament in June 1895. The Open Championship was to be played over the Old Course in that year, and the professional tournament was a complementary event. Sandy Herd, playing under the Huddersfield banner, won the first prize of £15 with two rounds of 86 for an aggregate of 172. Andra' Kirkaldy, the local professional, finished fourth, winning £4 10s, but he salvaged some pride by returning the lowest single-round score of 85.

The layout was favourably received, especially by the long hitters. The committee had adopted what had become a popular device for discouraging beginners and ladies who were starting to take an interest in the men's game. They had left the first 50 to 80 yards from each tee to grow rough and untended, to the extent that it was frightening to look at. But suddenly, in November 1895, a pony and a large mowing-machine appeared on the scene to cut the grass from tee to green. Mechanisation had arrived, even if it was only one horsepower.

Orn Hjartarson, the amateur from Iceland who set a new record of 60 for the New Course in the St Andrews Links Trophy, with the chairman of the organising committee, Robert Burns, on the left. Hjartarson had a 15-foot putt on the final green for a 59

A view of the town
across the Links

The first of the New Course amenities was provided in May 1907, when a wooden shelter was built by the R&A near the first tee. The R&A did their best to encourage play on the New Course, and to this end they transferred their annual tournament for the Calcutta Cup from the Old Course to the New Course. (In those days the tournament was contested by singles during the autumn meeting, and it did not become a foursomes event until 1921.)

With the advent of steel-shafted clubs in 1929 and improvements in the performance of golf balls, the Town Council and the R&A felt in 1938 that there were grounds for a reappraisal of the course's potential, and they called in Messrs Colt, Allison and Morrison Ltd to make the assessment. Mr H.S. Colt had already established a reputation in St Andrews by designing the popular Eden Course. The architects reported that the course could not be improved materially unless additional land could be utilised, in order to strengthen the finishing holes 14 to 18.

To add emphasis to the notion that a more testing course was needed if the status of St Andrews as a championship venue was to be maintained, a trio of golfing experts – Sir Guy Campbell, Major C.M. Hutchison and Sir Nairne Stewart Sandeman – had put forward proposals for a super-championship course. The Second World War, however, was only a few months away and the proposals were consigned to the archives.

The notion of making the New Course more testing surfaced again just after the millennium. A round on the New was an integral element in the increasingly prestigious Links Trophy event for top-class amateur golfers. With handicaps of scratch or better, usually the latter, they were finding the course a little short for a serious test, and consequently a 'championship' length was created. This was achieved by lengthening some of the holes, notably the 7th, 10th, 12th and 14th, and raising the total length by 160 to 6,781 yards.

In 2006, Welshman Nigel Edwards, playing in the Links Trophy, shot 64, seven under par, to establish the record for the newly lengthened layout.

THE JUBILEE COURSE

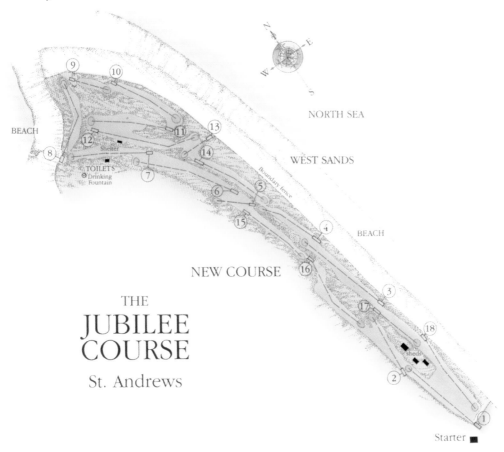

Although the construction by the local authority of a third course was not mentioned in the 1894 Links Act, it had always been the intention of the Town Council to provide a course where beginners and ladies could play and so relieve pressure on the other courses. In March 1897, a special committee which had been set up to examine the possibility of providing such a course reported that it was possible to construct a course of 12 holes on the seaward side of the New Course, and that it might be possible eventually to extend it to 18 holes. Within a month, the Town Council had an estimate from Mr John Angus Jr, who undertook to lay out the course and have it ready for play in the current season for £178 3s 8d. In less than a week, he had 20 men working on the course. Three weeks later, it was reported to the Town Council that the course would be ready for play on 22 June 1897, the day on which a public holiday was to be observed in St Andrews to mark the Diamond Jubilee of Queen Victoria. The council agreed that the course should be formally opened on that day and that it should be known as the Jubilee Course. The formal opening was performed by the wife of Provost

Charlie Ward (Little Aston), who partnered Jimmy Adams (Beaconsfield) in a four-ball exhibition match against local amateurs Andrew Dowie and Willie Mitchell in 1946 to mark the opening of the extended Jubilee Course (St Andrews University)

John Macgregor, and she was presented with a club made in Tom Morris's shop.

The layout of the course was fairly basic, which is hardly surprising, given the cost and the speed of its construction. The greens were nominal, and even in 1902 it was reported that it was more appropriate to use an iron or a mashie on the Jubilee greens than to use a putter. Repairs, too, when they were carried out, were primitive. When in 1902 something was needed to stop sand blowing over the course, the council solved the problem by setting 36 old railway sleepers near the first teeing ground.

At about the same time, David Honeyman, Tom Morris's right-hand man, suggested that the course might be extended to 18 holes, and this was done in 1905 at a cost of £150. As previously mentioned, agreement was reached with the commanders of the local Rifle and Artillery Volunteer Corps to regulate play when shooting was in progress at the butts and range at the far end of the course.

The first four and the last five holes of the course were on the landward side of the sand dunes, and this formed an easy and pleasant circuit for young people learning the game and for elderly people. The other nine holes were on the seaward side and to the north on rough, undeveloped ground, riddled with rabbit warrens and to a great extent overgrown by rough, bent grass.

Not everybody approved of the changes made to the Links to create the Jubilee Course. In 1907, Dr John H. Wilson, a distinguished naturalist and founder of St Andrews University's Botanic Gardens, complained about the planting of whins on the sand dunes on the Jubilee Course. He argued that the whin bushes, viewed from the Elysian Fields on the Old Course had 'been an eyesore for a number of years', and he maintained that if nature had wanted whin bushes on the sand dunes, nature would have put them there. It was painfully evident that they had been *planted* there.

Police Judge Andrew Balsillie, a member of the Town Council, explained that when the R&A laid out the New Course they had destroyed the whin bushes which adorned the central part of the Links, and the Town Council was trying to redress the wrong. He added: 'Besides the delight they offer to the eye, the whins provide a home for feathered and insect life which appeals to other interests and to other senses of the human family.' The whins continue to grace the Jubilee Course.

In 1929, the Town Council again sought the advice of Mr H.S. Colt, who was impressed by the 'large area of very delightful sand dune country available for alteration to the course'. But it needed a lot of work. The Town Council made no decision at the time, fearing that the cost might be higher than they were prepared to pay. They were just as wary in 1938, when they called in Mr Colt's company to have another look, but they did agree that at the end of the current season they would make a start on the reconstruction of the course using local labour under the supervision of Willie Auchterlonie, the 1893 Open champion, who was honorary professional to the R&A. War put a brake on the operation – manpower and material were in short supply – but the work crawled on, with Willie having to depart from time to time from the guidelines laid down by Mr Colt.

In February 1946, only a few months after the end of the war, the Town Council was able to report that the course was nearing completion. In June of the same year, the course was formally opened by Willie striking a ball from the first tee. This was followed by an inaugural exhibition match featuring two prominent professionals, Jimmy Adams (Beaconsfield) and Charlie Ward (Little Aston), and two local amateurs, Andrew Dowie and W.B.G. Mitchell.

The course, 6,020 yards long, still required much work and it had not been fully bunkered. Willie was characteristically modest about his achievement. He gave the credit to the town's greenkeeping staff and said that what had been accomplished 'was just another step towards the creation of a top-class course'. And he made this prediction: 'It won't be in my day, but some day this will be a championship course.' Willie died in 1963 at the age of 91.

The opening of the Forth and Tay road bridges in the 1960s put additional pressure on the St Andrews courses by opening the door to golfers from the major population centres of Dundee and Edinburgh. The Town Council decided to call in golf course architects Hawtree and Sons to look at proposals for redesigning the Jubilee Course and the New Course to provide starting points which might serve more than one circuit of nine holes. The architects produced a comprehensive report but they warned: 'A solution designed for summer which condemned regular players to inconvenience for the rest of the year is not acceptable. The compromise must cover domestic factors and not lean too strongly towards the comfort of visitors alone.' The Hawtree Report was an excellent assessment of the problems which faced St Andrews Town Council in their efforts to improve and extend golfing facilities in the town, but the council felt that by implementing any of the alternatives put forward they would be creating as many problems as they might solve.

TOP LEFT: The second green of the redesigned Jubilee Course presents a narrow target for the second shot

TOP RIGHT: The homeward holes on the Jubilee Course provide a good view of the town

LEFT: Donald Steel's redesign of the course created a much tougher proposition, as the narrow, part-blind approach to the 15th green shows

The situation was compounded by the need to provide practice facilities for championship events. The R&A Championship Committee in 1982 had cast a covetous eye over the first and 18th fairways of the Jubilee Course as a suitable area but the Links Trust did not favour the sterilisation of the ground for the sake of an event which might be staged at St Andrews once in six years.

The Trust and the Championship Committee compromised in 1983 when the Trust agreed that the starting and finishing area of the Jubilee could be adapted as a practice area for major events, as the Jubilee Course was, in any case, closed during these competitions.

This proposal ran in parallel with plans to upgrade the Jubilee Course to championship standard. The design was entrusted to the golf course architects Cotton, Pennink, Steel and Partners, and in particular to Mr Donald Steel, who was quick to spot the area's golfing and scenic potential. Mr Steel raised the teeing areas so that uninterrupted views of the sea and the landward area were exposed. This process assisted his other objective, for it opened up the course and exposed the players to the fierce winds which sweep across the North Sea and which make even the more sheltered Old Course a really tough proposition.

One of the problems which plagued the Jubilee was the liability of some of the fairways to flooding. In 1988, the Trust sought the help of Barry F. Cooper, who introduced a system which siphons off surface water to a storage tank, from where it can be used in course irrigation. Mr Steel produced a golf course of 6,805 yards – more than 500 yards longer than the old Jubilee – and made skilful use of the sand dunes without causing any noticeable alteration to the well-known skyline.

The redesigned course was opened for play in July 1989, but the official opening was not performed until the end of September of that year, when Curtis Strange, the US Open champion, drove a ball from the first tee. He was invited to perform the opening because he held the record score of 62 for the Old Course, and he was in St Andrews as a member of the US team for the 1989 Dunhill Tournament. The course had the usual medal and 'friendly' tees for men and women players, but in 1992 the Trust introduced Bronze teeing grounds.

They took this step because local club players found the Jubilee, even from the friendly tees, a really tough proposition. The Trust agreed, but the course had been designed to be a real test of golf. The new Bronze teeing grounds were sympathetically located to take the worst of the bite out of the course during winter when playing conditions are most severe. They were recognised as forming an official circuit of the course with its own standard scratch score so that it could be used for club medal competitions.

THE EDEN COURSE

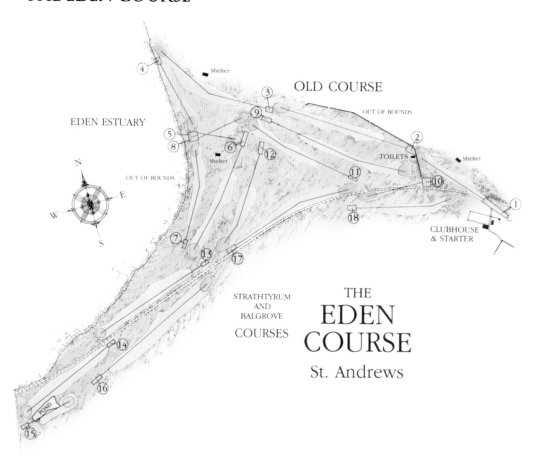

The Eden Course came into being after the passing of the 1913 Act. As described in an earlier chapter, the area on which the course was constructed included ground lying to the south of the 12th fairway of the Old Course which already belonged to the Town Council and was heavily covered by whins and gorse, two fields lying to the south of the railway line, and three fields lying between the railway line and the Old Course, all belonging to James Cheape of Strathtyrum. The council leased the ground initially for 25 years at a rental of £130 a year.

The Town Council engaged Mr H.S. Colt of Sunningdale to design the course. It was his first venture in golf course design in St Andrews, although he knew the Links well as a member of the R&A, having twice won its Jubilee Vase tournament, in 1891 and 1893, playing off scratch. He had a considerable reputation as a golf course architect, having laid out Sunningdale, although Willie Park had been responsible for some of the early layout. He had also designed Swinley Forest, which was considered to be the model on which many other courses were based. His international reputation was enhanced by the counsel and assistance which he gave to the Philadelphia sportsman George Crump, who laid out Pine Valley in Clementon, New Jersey, reckoned to be one of the world's finest courses. His man on the spot was Claude Harris, also based at Sunningdale, who carried out the work on the Eden using local labour.

The course followed the line which it was to occupy for the next three-quarters of a century. There were many natural plateaux, which provided ideal conditions for putting, and only two artificial greens had to be contrived. There were originally 61 bunkers dotted throughout the course.

The formal opening was on Saturday, 4 July 1914, when Mrs Herkless, wife of Provost John Herkless, hit the first drive. The ball was later mounted in silver and preserved in the showcase in St Andrews Town Hall. Mrs Herkless was presented with a silver cup to mark the occasion, but all trace of this memento was lost for many years. It was eventually discovered in an antique shop in England and purchased for £200 by St Andrews Links Trust in 1985. Since then, it has been contested among members of the ladies' golf clubs in St Andrews.

Crowds crossing the bridge which straddled the railway line bisecting the Eden Course

The old shepherd's cottage that sits behind the 1st green of the Eden Course

The opening ceremony was also marked by a match between local golfers and members of the R&A. The suggestion came from Councillor John Reid, who felt that a match between the R&A and a 'Team of Local Talent' would do much to foster good relations between the club and the town. It proved to be such a good idea that after the First World War the match was revived with the 'Team o' Talent', as the town's team came to be known, meeting a team of R&A members each year over the Old Course during the club's autumn meeting.

The opening match in 1914 was played over only 15 holes of the Eden Course, for the fifth, sixth and seventh holes, which had been laid out over land which had to be cleared of dense whins, were still immature. The match was played by foursomes with 34 players on each side, and it resulted in a win for the R&A members by 7 games to 6 and 4 halved.

The reduction in play caused by the First World War, which broke out only a month after the formal opening, helped the process of consolidation of the course, particularly the three holes which had been cleared of whin bushes.

When the war ended, the Town Council started to think of ways of maximising the use of the course and at the same time encouraging people to come to St Andrews for holidays. It was decided that an open amateur tournament should be held, and so the Eden Tournament was born in 1920. It was to become one of the most important events in the Scottish calendar, taking second place only to the Scottish Amateur Championship. Success in 'the Eden' was often followed by international recognition.

The Town Council had, for many years, harboured ideas about buying the course – or at least that part of it which was leased from Mr Cheape. They had considered it in 1923 but went no further. In 1936, the idea came up again, and an approach was made to Mr Cheape, who agreed to feu 80.622 acres of land for an annual feu duty of £302 6s 8d (which works out at £3.75 per acre). The feu contract was signed on 16 December 1936, and Mr Cheape specified that the lands 'shall only be used as a public park and place of public resort and recreation or for a golf course and shall not be used for any other purpose'.

Two years later, the Town Council called in Mr Colt to suggest how the course might be improved. There had been little or no call for change, and local opinion confirmed that no change was needed. One suggestion made by Mr Colt was that at the 17th hole any ball played over the fence and wall should be out of bounds, and this was adopted by the Town Council.

The 144-yard 5th hole on the Eden Course, where a local golfer holed in one using his putter from the tee

Hares are a common sight on the Links. They are so used to golfers that they only move if there is a risk of a really close encounter

The Eden Course became probably the most popular of the St Andrews courses. It was by no means the most challenging, but it was a pleasant, scenic, holiday course which suited many of the older players who found the Old and the New too long and testing. It reached its full potential after 1969, when the St Andrews –Leuchars branch railway line was closed and players were relieved of the burden of carrying clubs and caddie carts over the wooden bridge which had straddled the railway line beside the second green. The Town Council installed overhead irrigation sprinklers on the tees and greens in 1971 at a cost of £9,542.

Change came not through any public demand, nor from any sense that the course was inadequate; it stemmed from the need to provide suitable facilities for practice and an area which could be used for the tented village by the R&A Championship Committee during major events. The Championship Committee had, in 1983, expressed interest through the Links Trust in an area of 20 acres belonging to Mrs Gladys Cheape who was, by that time, proprietress of Strathtyrum Estate. Mrs Cheape was at first reluctant to part with any of her land but negotiations continued, and in 1986 Sir John Carmichael, chairman of the Links Trust, announced that 118 acres of Strathtyrum Estate had been acquired – all of it contiguous with the existing courses.

In considering proposals for the use of the land, the Links Management Committee unanimously approved a plan for the first, second, 17th and 18th fairways of the Eden to be given over to a driving range and practice area which could be used for the tented village during championships. They urged the Trustees to agree. The R&A offered to pay the costs of a study into the uses of all the new land and into the Links Management Committee's plans for the Eden.

The Trust engaged the golf course architects Cotton, Pennink, Steel and Partners to draw up alternative plans for the comprehensive use of the newly acquired land and possible redevelopment of the Eden and Balgove courses. Both plans made provision for a replacement nine-hole Balgove Course, a new short 18-hole course to be known as the Strathtyrum Course, and a driving range and practice facilities. The main difference between the two plans was that in the first the Eden Course was to remain unchanged; and in the second, the first, second, 17th and 18th holes were to be redeveloped for the driving range and practice facilities and the holes lost on the Eden Course were to be replaced by new holes to be formed on the newly acquired land.

The Links Trust asked the local golf clubs for their views, and only the St Andrews Golf Club showed a preference for the first plan, which would have left the Eden Course untouched. When the issue came before the Links Trust for a final decision on 16 November 1987, they decided by five votes to two (with the chairman, Sir John Carmichael, abstaining) to go ahead with the second plan. The architects were then given the green light to proceed with the plan to take over the first, second, 17th and 18th fairways for the driving range and practice area and, when necessary, the tented village.

The new-look Eden Course was opened for play towards the end of 1989. The arrangements had the effect of centralising the Links administration at Pilmour Cottage, of which the Links Trust had taken a lease from the owners of the Old Course Hotel. The Trust went a step further in November 1990 when they announced that they had acquired Pilmour Cottage from the hotel in exchange for a 99-year lease of a parcel of ground at the far end of the new practice ground and including the original Eden Pavilion.

The 1989 remodelling of the Eden Course was a remarkable echo of a proposal initiated in 1973 by the Joint Links Committee before the passing of the 1974 Links Act. The subject was raised publicly in the Town Council by Bailie David Niven, who claimed that the Joint Links Committee had held consultations with Mr C.D. Lawrie on proposals to convert the first, second, 17th and 18th fairways into a practice ground and to incorporate part of the Balgove Course into a redesigned Eden Course. Bailie Niven claimed that the Town Council, as owners of the course, should have been consulted before any discussions were held.

This was followed by a public statement from Provost J.B. Gilchrist, who explained that it was a plan put forward by Mr Lawrie, a golf course architect, a member of the R&A, and a distinguished golfer. He had made the preliminary survey at his own expense, and it would have been discourteous if the Joint Links Committee had not listened to him. Mr Lawrie was told by the Town Council members of the Joint Links Committee what the local reaction would be to his proposals, and that the ladies' clubs in particular would most strongly object to walking to the third hole before starting play. Personally, he would deplore the loss of these four holes and the use of the pavilion but, on the other hand, there was an urgent need for a satisfactory practice ground. The Joint Links Committee had invited Mr Lawrie to prepare a written description of his proposals.

Before any decision was taken, the 1974 Act became law and negotiations passed to the Links Trust and Management Committee. But reorganisation of local government had not yet taken place, and the Town Council was still the local authority and, as such, the proprietor of the Links.

After consulting local golfers, the Town Council informed the Links Trust that they were opposed to the proposals, that the loss of the children's course, the Balgove, would be a retrograde step, and that a larger practice area would be an advantage but not at the expense of other, more popular facilities. And so the proposals were abandoned – or perhaps just postponed.

The redesigned Eden Course had a yardage of 6,423, with four par five holes and four par three holes giving a par of 72 – the same as the Old Course. Subsequent alterations and adjustments, however, reduced the length to 6,250 yards and the par to 70.

THE BALGOVE COURSE

With the post-war upgrading of the Jubilee Course, more and more adults were using the course which youngsters, until then, had regarded as their province.

The Town Council recognised that there was a need for a children's or learners' course, as this would keep both the children and the adults happy. In the late 1960s, the Junior Golf Club organised by parents and well-wishers bombarded the Town Council with the problems facing children who had a genuine interest in the game. The council looked for land but there was none on the seaward side and the land to the south belonged to

Strathtyrum Estate. An early attempt to purchase a part of Strathtyrum known as Balgove had failed, but the Town Council tried again in 1971, and in September of that year Mrs Gladys Cheape agreed to sell for £12,150. The area extended to 26.84 acres, which was big enough for a safe nine-hole course, but any hope of extending the small practice area had to be shelved.

One snag about the field was that access to Balgove was possible only by using the old Mussel Road, which skirted the 17th fairway of the Old Course and then cut across the 17th fairway of the Eden Course. This was an extremely hazardous passage for young children, so the Town Council constructed a new access road from the old Guardbridge Road.

The Balgove Course – nine holes, stretching to 2,085 yards – was opened in February 1972. It was to have a short life, for part of it was taken over in the 1989–90 remodelling of the Eden Course, and the Links Trust gave a promise that a redesigned Balgove Course would be constructed in the future. Plans for the new course were announced by the Trust in September 1990, showing that it was to have nine holes, a length of 1,700 yards and a par of 31.

The course was constructed at the same time as the new 18-hole course, the Strathtyrum, and it was opened on 20 June 1993 at 5 p.m. by the members of the St Andrews Children's Golf Club. It had had to be shortened slightly, to 1,520 yards, and the par reduced to 30, but to the children it was a 'real' course with proper tees, greens and even two greenside bunkers. The old Balgove had been little more than a field, and the contrast was obvious.

Children on the Balgove Course (Masakuni Akiyama)

The green on the
2nd hole of the
Balgove Course

In the event, in its early years the course proved so popular with adults as well as children that the Links Management Committee decided to introduce a special rule temporarily during the school summer holidays to the effect that adults could only play the Balgove if accompanied by a child.

THE STRATHTYRUM COURSE

The 18-hole Strathtyrum Course, which had originally been planned with a yardage of 5,105, finished very close to the plan at 5,094 yards. It was designed to meet the needs of young developers in the game and older people who just wanted a quiet, easy round. With a par of 69 and only 11 bunkers, the course was opened for play on 1 July 1993, the first 18-hole course to open at St Andrews for 79 years. The first players to tee off were Jock Steven, a local farmer and president of the Scottish Rugby Union, and his son Ian, who were the winners of a competition run through the columns of the local newspaper, the *St Andrews Citizen*.

The Donald Steel-designed course soon became a popular choice of local people. It was fairly flat, and it became the favourite of elderly golfers and those who wanted a quick round. Many were surprised that they could complete 18 holes of golf in little over two-and-a-half hours.

Sir John Carmichael (right), chairman of the Links Trust, in 1986 negotiated the purchase of 118 acres of land from the Strathtyrum estate. He is seen here receiving the 1973 Bing Crosby Trophy from Professor J.A. Macdonald, captain of the New Golf Club (St Andrews University)

Bunkers in the 1890s were not as neatly manicured as they were a hundred years later (George Washington Wilson Collection)

In the early days of its life, the course was fringed by rough which tended to be rather punitive, but the Management Committee, recognising that it was intended to be a relaxing course, took the obvious remedial measures. As an additional aid for the elderly and golfers with some disability, the Trust permitted buggies to be used over the Strathtyrum Course. In 2004, medal tees were introduced by the Links Management Committee and the number of bunkers increased to 15. This new medal length added over 500 yards to the existing length, making the course a significantly tougher proposition, especially if the prevailing westerly wind was blowing with any strength.

With the opening of the Strathtyrum and Balgove courses, the number of holes available for golfers at St Andrews rose to 99, making it the largest golf complex in Europe.

THE CASTLE COURSE

Early in 1998, proposals were being put forward by developers to add almost one third to St Andrews' housing stock and, consequently, to its population. This would be certain to result in a substantial increase in demand for play on the Links courses, which were already full at popular times. Trustees were concerned.

The reason for the concern was that over 90 per cent of the Links' revenue was generated from golfing visitors, who played less than 45 per cent of the golf. Less than 10 per cent of revenue required to finance the running of the courses came from local golfers, who played around 55 per cent of the golf. Trustees were conscious of their responsibilities to residents, but if the delicate balance between visitor play and local play was seriously upset, the Links' financial stability could be in jeopardy. The alternative of imposing huge increases on the traditionally low local charges to compensate for a major reduction in visitor revenue was considered unacceptable. Equally unacceptable was another option of reducing drastically the number of yearly tickets issued to club members who did not reside in the town, so as to create the extra capacity for the new residents.

The Trustees set up a working party to look in detail at demand trends and at how much play the courses could withstand while remaining in high-quality condition.

The result of the working party's analysis was that the existing six courses could withstand a maximum of 220,000 rounds of golf in total each year. Independent experts from the Sports Turf Research Institute endorsed this figure. In 1998, 208,000 rounds were played, and all the signs indicated that growth would continue. The working party concluded that, if nothing was done, in five years' time demand would exceed capacity and the 'full up' sign would have to be hung out.

The Trustees were not inclined simply to throw away the improvements that had been made in the playing conditions over the last few years by allowing greatly increased play on the courses, with a consequent reduction in course quality. While some measures could be introduced to restrict the growth in demand in the short term, the Trustees were conscious that if they were to meet their obligations to residents and remain financially sound, the only real answer for the long term was to increase capacity. This meant another golf course. But how was this to be achieved?

A variety of options were considered, such as joint ventures with other local course owners, buying one of the other local courses, or building another course. In the end, in the light of legal advice, and for reasons of practicality, the other options were ruled out, and the Trustees decided to start from scratch and create a new course, even though it had only been five years since the Strathtyrum Course had opened for play.

This approach was seen as having a number of advantages: the course could be built to the Trust's standards with no short cuts; it could be designed in the way the Trust wanted; and it would be solely under the Trust's control, enabling it to be run similarly to the existing six courses – in other words, with the same favourable pricing and access for locals that characterised the present arrangements for the Links. Visitors would pay a commercial rate and their access would be similar to that on the existing courses. The disadvantage was that building a new course would take time.

A meeting with the local golf clubs and other interests in the town was convened in November 1998, and the Trustees explained the problem and their thinking. Broad support for both the short-term restrictive measures and the long-term solution was forthcoming, but when the question of where the new course would be located was raised, there was not, as yet, an answer.

There was no available land left on the Links, so new land would have to be found. The first place to look was as near to the existing courses as possible, and the next three years were spent trying to reach agreement with Strathtyrum Estate, the long-time, co-operative, next-door neighbour of the Links. Times had changed, however. Gladys Cheape, the proprietress who had sold to the Trust the land for the Strathtyrum Course, and, in 1993, had sold the famous Cheape rights back to the Trust, had died. The estate had passed to a trust, and the plans of the estate trustees did not fit in with the plans of the Links Trust. An alternative would have to be found.

The alternative emerged when one of the Trustees advised the Trust's general manager that he believed some land might be available for purchase on the east side of town, about four miles from the existing Links. A visit to the site revealed an area of sloping farmland in a spectacular clifftop setting overlooking St Andrews, which looked as though it would make an ideal location for a golf course.

Agreement was reached with the farmer, Sandy Fyfe, and with his western neighbour, John Raeside, from whom a smaller parcel of land was required, and the tortuous process of gaining planning approval got under way in 2002. After spending almost two years and over £100,000 on the professional specialists necessary to meet the planners' requirements, the Trust submitted its planning application in late 2003.

RIGHT: The spectacular position of The Castle Course overlooking St Andrews (Larry Lambrecht)

Opposition to the application had been mounted from a variety of groups. Unsurprisingly, some commercial operators of other courses nearby, who perhaps saw a competitive threat, objected, along with some non-golfing individuals who considered that there was already too much focus on golf in the town. More surprisingly, perhaps, St Andrews Community Council objected, as did a small number of local golfers and some local hoteliers. The Community Council for the district around the village of Boarhills, in whose area the course was to be built, was entirely supportive, however, and neither the St Andrews Green Belt Forum nor the Preservation Trust objected.

At a special meeting of the local authority's planning committee on a wet February evening in 2004 in the Boarhills village hall, the objectors were encouraged to state their case and the Trust was asked to respond. The result was that planning approval was granted, subject to the Trust meeting 27 conditions before work could get under way. It took until November that year to satisfy the planners that the conditions either had been or would be met, and the go-ahead was given.

While the planning process was grinding its way through, architects for the new golf course, and for the associated buildings, had been appointed and had been beavering away on their detailed plans. When it had been announced that a seventh course was being planned at the 'Home of Golf' and a firm of golf course architects to design it was being sought, some 20 such firms from around the world had expressed serious interest. They saw clearly that being chosen to design a new course at St Andrews Links would be a very considerable feather in their caps. In the end, six firms were interviewed, and the choice fell on David Kidd and his company, DMK Design.

Kidd was young, Scottish and had shot to fame by designing the acclaimed Bandon Dunes course on America's west coast. Importantly, he had guaranteed a hands-on approach and had committed to having his chief designer, Paul Kimber, permanently on site during the construction process. Not only did this provide the close supervision required for ensuring a high quality of work, but it also kept costs down by avoiding the need for a main contractor: both matters of great interest to the Trust.

Almost the first action of the architects after surveying the site was to ask the Trust to buy more land. They had seen that an additional short stretch of coastline would enable them to create a spectacular par three hole, adding significantly to the appeal of the course. This was agreed, as well as the purchase of another small strip of land from Scottish Water that would improve the routing of the new course.

The Trust had laid down only a few constraints for the architects – apart from the obvious one of cost. The main constraints were that the course had to be enjoyable to play, there were to be short distances to walk from green to tee, and there should be five tees on every hole so that all levels of golfers could play without feeling that it demanded shots beyond their capability. At the same time it was to be no 'walk in the park', but was to provide a challenge for the variety of golfers expected to play the course.

Construction started on 1 April 2005 with the aim of opening for play in 2007. A particularly wet spring, however, delayed progress, so that by November only five holes had been seeded, and it was recognised that the course would not be ready for 2007. Fortunately, good weather in 2006 enabled almost all the remaining seeding to take place, with the final touches applied in spring 2007. The greenkeepers for the new course, most of whom had been on-board throughout the construction process, were now able to get to work to ensure that grass flourished on fairways, the greens were smooth and true, and the rough was not too penal, in time for the rescheduled opening in June 2008.

In parallel with the course construction, the buildings architect, Fraser Smart, had worked on the design of the course maintenance facilities, the entrance road and the clubhouse. Tenders were put out for the building of these elements, and the successful firm for all three contracts was Clachan Construction.

As far as the important matter of finance for the project was concerned, a loan facility from the Trust's bankers was put in place, to which the R&A generously added an interest-free loan. The rest was to come from the Trust's surpluses.

The 18th green of The Castle Course (Larry Lambrecht)

While the course was ready for play early in 2008, it could not be opened until the clubhouse was completed, and this was finally achieved at the last gasp, after the builders had pulled out all the stops, in the last week of June that year.

The official opening of The Castle Course – the name chosen from 4,000 submissions to a worldwide naming competition run through the Links' website – was performed by HRH The Duke of York on 2 July 2008, when he unveiled a plaque at the first tee. The first drive following the unveiling was struck by Edwin Burtnett of Tampa, Florida, who had won the naming competition.

St Andrews residents now had seven courses at their disposal, although the 2008 price for the yearly ticket to play all seven caused a furore by rising £40 from £125 for six courses in 2007.

TOP LEFT: The 12th green

ABOVE: HRH The Duke of York declares The Castle Course officially open

The new course was unlike any of the Links courses, with more penal rough demanding greater accuracy of shot-making, and some severely sloping greens. Some golfers felt their golf was not up to it, but others became instant fans. Minor 'tweaking' of some of the course's features was agreed between the Trust and the architects in places where the first four months of play had shown it was advisable, and this was carried out in its closure period during the winter of 2008–9.

The Castle Course quickly attracted awards from around the world. It was awarded the accolade of '2008 Turf Professional Project of the Year' by a panel of greenkeeping experts; it was named the 'New Course of the Year' by *Travel+Leisure Golf* magazine in the USA; it was designated the 'International Development of the Year' by *Golf Inc*, another US golf publication; and it was ranked by *Golf World* in its top 100 courses. David Kidd was recognised too by being named as the 'Golf Course Architect of the Year' by *Golf* magazine. All were agreed that St Andrews had a spectacular addition to its golfing stock.

The Castle Course at sunset

PROTECTION FROM THE SEA

Proximity to the sea is an essential component of links golf, but the risk of erosion always threatens its very existence. At St Andrews that risk had been apparent for a number of years and was a constant source of concern.

The most vulnerable stretches of coastline were along the banks of the Eden Estuary. The 12th tee of the Old Course, the 9th of the New Course, the 8th of the Jubilee and the 4th and 7th fairways of the Eden Course, had all presented problems which had been solved by shielding them with gabions – metal cages filled with stones. These had, in the course of time, become colonised by the sand-binding marram grass. This strengthened the defensive powers of the gabions and made them less obtrusive. In 1999 the Trust doubled the amount spent on these defences to £90,000. However, one length of coastline – about 400 metres alongside the 8th fairway of the Jubilee – seemed to be particularly vulnerable.

Sunset over the Eden Estuary, where erosion threatens the Links

The head greenkeeper of the Jubilee Course inspects erosion after the storm

In the autumn of 1999, the Links Trust sought planning permission to place more gabions along this stretch, which was eroding so rapidly as to cause real concern. To the dismay of the Trust, approval was withheld to enable a study to be carried out. The trouble was that that part of the coastline on the Eden Estuary was an ecologically sensitive area and registered as a Site of Special Scientific Interest. An independent study was carried out by the Links Trust in association with Scottish Natural Heritage, Fife Council and the Ministry of Defence. The MOD was involved because of the interests of RAF Leuchars on the other side of the Estuary.

After this study had taken place, and with the sea lapping only a few yards from the Jubilee's 8th fairway and parts of coastal footpath washed away, planning permission was granted in the autumn of 2000.

The Trust adopted two measures to repair the damage and halt the erosion. Stone-filled metal gabions were placed along 100 metres of unprotected dunes between the Estuary and the Links: they were sloping gabions rather than the vertical type used farther south. This was supplemented by replenishing the dunes with 12,000 cubic metres of sand.

In carrying out this remedial plan the Trust was looking after the interests not only of golfers but also the Estuary's wildlife. Birds which feed and breed there include the reed bunting, skylark, short-eared owl, meadow pipit, wren and many others. It was not a random bonus accruing from the

Coastal protection
work. Gabions
being installed in
winter 2000

Coastal protection work. Gabions being installed in winter 2000

anti-erosion works, but arose from consultations carried out with Scottish Natural Heritage, Fife Council Ranger Service and the Roads Department, the RSPB, the Sea Mammal Research Institute, the Scottish Environment Protection Agency and St Andrews University.

In addition to the £90,000 spent on the gabions in 1999, the new measures cost in the region of £200,000.

Constant monitoring of the success of the measures was undertaken, which revealed that the gabions were entirely successful, but that the additional sand which had been used to replenish the beaches was being eroded. This necessitated sand replenishment in 2001 and 2008, and it was apparent that this would be a recurrent activity – and a not insubstantial cost – every six or seven years.

THE HOLES AND BUNKERS
OF THE OLD COURSE

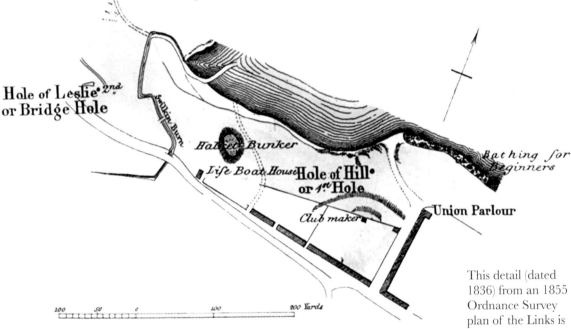

Fac simile of part of Plan of the Golfing Course over the Links of St. Andrews, surveyed by order of The Royal St. Andrews Golfing Society, by W. & J. Chalmers, Perth 1836. In possession of St. Mary's College.

Hole of Leslie 2nd or Bridge Hole

Halket Bunker

Swilken Burn

Life Boat House

Club maker

Hole of Hill or 1st Hole

Bathing for Beginners

Union Parlour

100   50   0   100   200 Yards

A ny dissertation on the names of the holes on the Old Course must be open to question, for very little documented evidence is available; indeed, some holes appear from time to time to have swapped names, some have changed and some have disappeared.

The holes which are presently referred to by old names are the original outward holes – now the inward holes. Looking at the holes on their original circuit, the first hole from the first tee to the present 17th green has been variously known as the Hole o' Hill, Hole o' Leslie and the Bridge Hole. The Hole o' Hill probably got its name from one of the old teeing grounds on Witch Hill, which lies to the east of the 18th green. Hole o' Leslie may have come from Captain Thomas Leslie, who was MP for the burgh from 1743 to 1761 or (less likely) from the Hon. George Waldegrove Leslie, who

This detail (dated 1836) from an 1855 Ordnance Survey plan of the Links is one of the few maps showing Halket's bunker. It is also interesting to note that the width of the first and 18th fairways was only 85 yards. By 1855 this had increased to 135 yards. The detail also shows the Lifeboat House and the Union Parlour

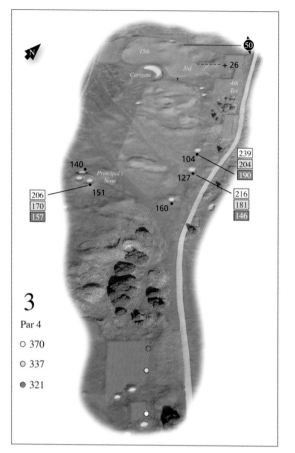

3

Par 4

○ 370

○ 337

● 321

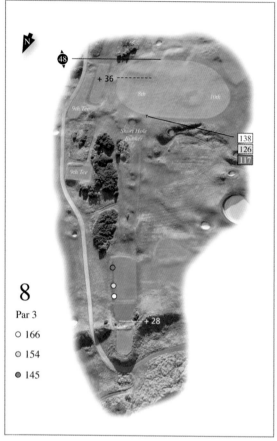

8

Par 3

○ 166

○ 154

● 145

ABOVE LEFT:
Cartgate Out

ABOVE RIGHT:
Short Hole

captained the R&A in 1878. The Bridge Hole obviously got its name from the old stone footbridge over the Swilcan which is so old that no one can tell how or when it originated.

The old second hole has been known as the Corner o' the Dyke and Balfield Hole. The corner of the dyke is a feature of the old wall which forms the boundary between the Old Course Hotel and the 17th fairway. Balfield, or Ba'field, is a corruption of Ballfield, and this name doubtless originated from the area to the south of the green which was a sports field for two local boarding schools and for students of St Andrews University. Many towns in Scotland have streets or areas known as Ba'field, Ballfield or Bellfield, and most of these have, at some time, had associations with ball-related games.

The third hole was, and still is, known as Cartgate because it was close to the road track which crossed the fairway giving access to the West Sands.

The fourth hole has been known as Cunnin' Links because the only line of play was down a narrow, whin-lined fairway which gave sanctuary to rabbits, or *cuniggis* as they were known in old Scots. Nowadays, the hole is known as the Ginger Beer Hole for it was here that Old Daw Anderson had his mobile refreshment stall dispensing ginger beer – and, if you were in the know, something a little more potent.

Old Daw had a hand in providing the name for the fifth hole, which was known as the Hole o' Cross. Some writers claim that it took its name from the chasm, knee deep in whins, heather and rough grass, which players had to *cross* in their approach to the green. Just as likely an explanation is that the fifth green was the first to have two holes cut on it – one for the outgoing players and the other for the incoming players. This was an innovation introduced by Old Daw when he was custodian of the Links. The hole assumed the title the Hole Across, and this was subsequently corrupted to the Hole o' Cross. Nowadays, the hole is referred to as the Long Hole Out or the Long Hole In, depending upon whether you are playing the fifth or 14th. Some of the holes share a name with their parallel neighbour.

The sixth hole was known as Muir Hole, Heathery Hole or Hole o' Shell. The hole was heavily covered by heather, and this could have given rise to either of the first two names. The Hole o' Shell came from the green, which was completely devoid of grass – in the early days it consisted of shelly sand rolled flat on top of a soft, spongy carpet of heather fibre.

The seventh hole was the High Hole because of the commanding position of the green overlooking the Eden Estuary. It is marked on one map as Hole o' Rhi. There was no obvious reason for this short-lived name, unless it was the proliferation of the sand-binding marram grass, which is not unlike rye in appearance and which aided the reclamation of the ground on which the new seventh green was constructed.

BELOW LEFT: The curling route of the Swilcan Burn takes it directly along the front edge of the 1st green (Masakuni Akiyama)

BELOW RIGHT: Boase bunker on the ninth hole (Masakuni Akiyama)

Probably the most feared bunker on the Old Course, this deep little pot sits in the front left of the Road Hole (17th) green. It has destroyed the chances of many a championship hopeful and many are the amateur and professional golfers who have putted into it from the front of the green

The eighth hole was the Short Hole for obvious reasons, and the ninth was the End Hole or Hole o' Turn because that was where the original course ended and the players turned to play the same holes back again. With the creation of the new circuit after the introduction of two holes on each green, some holes were left without names, but, as indicated earlier, they simply assumed the name of their neighbour.

The 17th adopted, appropriately, the name the Road Hole because of the old turnpike road which forms its southern boundary and has blighted the prospects of many a championship hopeful.

The regular summer crowd watch the play from behind the 18th green (Masakuni Akiyama)

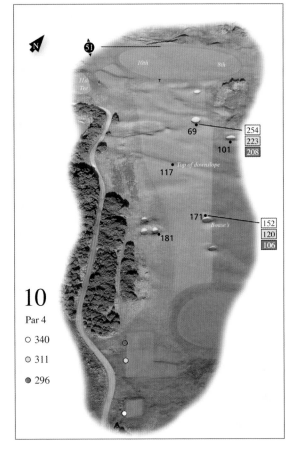

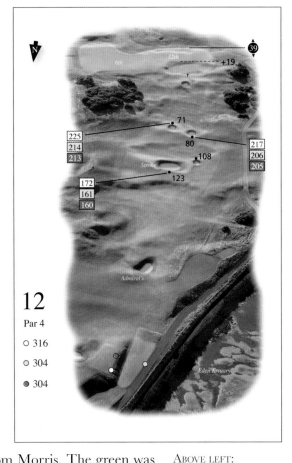

The 18th hole is now revered by the name Tom Morris. The green was constructed by Tom, and he regarded it as his finest work, watching it with pride from his shop window in Links Road.

For very many years the only hole without a name was the tenth. It became known from 1972 onwards as Bobby Jones in memory of the man who became a legend in St Andrews in his own lifetime. Bobby won the Open Championship at St Andrews in 1927 and the Amateur Championship in 1930 – the year of his Grand Slam. He returned to St Andrews in 1958 as non-playing captain of the United States team in the inaugural Eisenhower Trophy Match, and the town of St Andrews conferred on him the Freedom of the City.

Bobby died just before Christmas 1971, and in July of the following year, St Andrews Town Council agreed that the tenth hole of the Old Course should be named Bobby Jones in an act of remembrance of the great golfer. The service took place on Sunday, 10 September 1972, at the tenth tee. It was conducted by the Revd W.E.K. Rankin, honorary chaplain to the Royal and Ancient Golf Club. There was a gathering of about 200 people, including members of local golf clubs, St Andrews Town Council, and

ABOVE LEFT:
Bobby Jones

ABOVE RIGHT:
Heathery In

members of the public. The teeing box bearing Bobby's name was unveiled by Provost David Niven, and the blessing and closing prayer were given by the Revd Ian Paterson, Minister of Hope Park Church, St Andrews. As the congregation dispersed, a lament was played by Piper William Wotherspoon, a young St Andrean.

The bunkers with names and character are mostly those on the inward holes of the present-day Old Course. A sort of love–hate relationship developed between the golfers and the hazards, for the Scots, and particularly those of East Fife, delighted in bestowing nicknames on friend and foe alike, and it was often in the conviviality of claret and clubhouse that the bunkers of the Old Course gained their names.

One of the first bunkers encountered on the original Old Course was Halket's bunker, halfway down the first fairway. It was named after John Halket, who joined the Society of St Andrews Golfers in 1756. He was the rector of the local grammar school and became chaplain of the club in 1780. It remained a memorial to his name, or his exploits, for a number of years until it was filled in during the mid-nineteenth century when Sir Hugh Lyon Playfair was carrying out reclamation work on the first and 18th fairways.

In front of the old second tee at a distance of about 70 yards – on what is now the 17th fairway – is the Scholar's bunker, so called because it was a feather in the cap of young schoolboys if they were able to clear it with their drive. Farther on is a fairly deep bunker which used to be known as the Corner of the Dyke. It was later changed to Cheape's bunker as a mark of respect to the then owner of the Links – and possibly because it was less of a mouthful to pronounce.

Provost David Niven (right) and Bailie James Thompson (centre) unveil the tenth tee-box by removing the Scottish Saltire. On the left is the Revd W.E.K. Rankin, chaplain to the R&A, who dedicated the hole to the memory of Bobby Jones (G.M. Cowie)

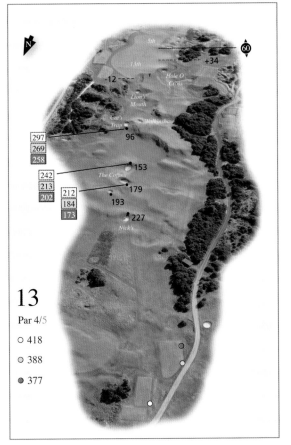

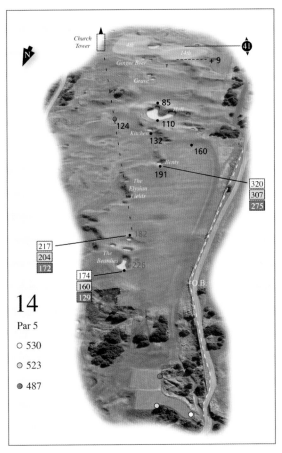

ABOVE LEFT:
Hole o' Cross

ABOVE RIGHT:
Long Hole

Beyond the green (now the 16th) is a nasty little bunker. It serves the dual purpose of catching a ball which overshoots the present second green and presenting a hazard against the approach to the 16th green. It is known as the Wig bunker. In the early days of golf, players had to be properly dressed for the game, which involved wearing a golfing jacket and, for some, a wig. The bunker's full name was Jackson's Wig, probably to mark the captaincy of Mr E.J. Jackson in 1852.

A short distance from the Wig on the old third fairway (now the 16th) is Grant's bunker, named after John Grant of Kilgraston, who captained the club in 1839. Not a long hitter, he was in his sixties and inclined to be a bit tubby, and he found the greatest difficulty in avoiding the bunker from the tee.

Progressing along the old third fairway, the player may encounter Deacon Sime, a nasty little pot which can trap the long hitter from the present-day 16th, provided he is able to avoid the Principal's Nose, that cluster of three bunkers – the nose and two nostrils – which must be among the most famous, or infamous, in the world of golf. There is a school of thought which points to Deacon Sime as a theologian, junior in rank to the principal, but it is

Cartgate bunker threatens approaches to the 3rd green that come from the left side of the fairway

more likely that he was a deacon of one of the Seven Incorporated Trades of St Andrews and therefore, *ex officio*, a member of the Town Council, or Police Commissioners as it was then known.

There are conflicting accounts of the origin of the name Principal's Nose. The most likely is that it owes its name to a rather ugly projecting porch on the house of the principal of St Andrews University in South Street. The porch was known as the Principal's Nose, and when it was demolished during the provostship of Sir Hugh Lyon Playfair, the name was transferred to the bunker. The other theory is that it was named after Principal Haldane, who was the principal of St Mary's College (the divinity school) of the university and who probably occupied the house with the ugly porch from 1800 to 1819. He was a prominent member of the R&A, and he officiated at the baptism of Old Tom Morris and later at his marriage to Agnes Bayne of Kincaple. Moreover, he was said to have had a rather prominent bulbous nose which achieved immortality in the bunker.

The huge greenside bunker at the third hole is called Cartgate because of its proximity to a cart track which led down to the sea.

Nearby was Tam's Coo, now filled in. Legend has it that a character known as Tam (or Tom) used to keep a milk cow tethered in that area. William Hodgson, in a remarkable flight of fancy in W.W. Tulloch's biography of Old Tom Morris, offers the suggestion that the Old Master was involved. He wrote:

Tom's natal origin was very peculiar. He was found one dewy morning in the 'Dyke Hole'. The date can be accurately ascertained from the fact that a bovine witness of the scene was so excited by its novelty as to have made the bunker known ever since as 'Tom's Coo'. The date of that performance will settle the date of Tom's origin.

In reality, Tom was born on 16 June 1821, the son of John Morris and Jean Bruce who hailed from the East Fife fishing burgh of Anstruther.

The filling up of Tom's Coo demonstrated the love–hate relationship which had grown up between the gentlemen golfers and the bunkers. George Glennie (whose memory is perpetuated in the Aggregate Medal which is contested over the R&A's spring and autumn meetings) turned out to witness the in-filling. The Revd Dr J.G. MacPherson wrote of that occasion: 'I remember old George Glennie looking sadly at the filling of Tom's Coo bunker as a knight of old would regard the dead body of an honoured and valiant rival; and he was the best golfer of his day.'

A short distance from the old fourth tee is a cluster of three small bunkers known as Rob's bunkers but no evidence has been found to identify Rob.

A little farther on is Sutherland, one of the best-known bunkers on the course. Sutherland was a flamboyant character, completely and utterly obsessed by golf. Golf was his whole life; anyone who had no knowledge of or interest in the game was 'an ignorant lout'. Of medium height, straight backed, square shouldered, and wearing the 'Scotch cap', the golfing

Cartgate bunker also punishes over hit approaches to the 15th green

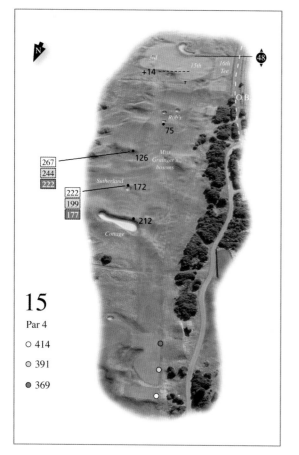

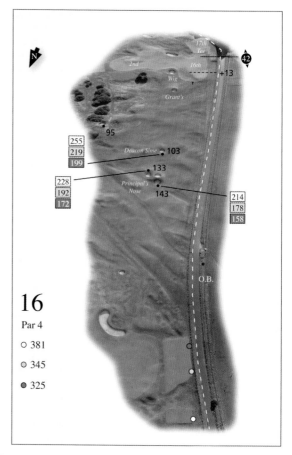

15

Par 4

○ 414

◉ 391

● 369

16

Par 4

○ 381

◉ 345

● 325

ABOVE LEFT:
Cartgate In

ABOVE RIGHT:
Corner o' the Dyke

headgear of the times, he looked more like a soldier than the lawyer he was. For A.G. Sutherland was a writer to the signet, which means that he was a solicitor entitled to conduct cases at the Court of Session. Whether he practised his profession widely is not clear, for he spent his winters on the Links at Musselburgh and his summers in St Andrews.

He got involved with the bunker which now bears his name in August 1869. He walked over the course one day and discovered that the bunker had been filled in. He wrote to Major Boothby, convener of the R&A's Green Committee, asking if the bunker had been filled in on the authority of the committee, and at the same time reminding him that the committee had no power to remove any bunker from the course. He suggested that the committee should restore the bunker to its former state or answer for their action in a court of law.

Major Boothby replied that he was not aware of any special orders having been given by the committee for filling up the bunker, but Tom Morris, as Custodian of the Links, had taken the opinion of many golfers who considered that the bunker was unnecessary. He added that he approved of the bunker being filled in, and he considered that if the committee wanted to close a bunker, they were within their rights to do so.

Sutherland was furious. He denied that Tom had the right 'to destroy or remodel the links as it pleases him and his clique', and he repeated his conviction that neither the R&A, the Green Committee, nor even the proprietor of the Links had the right to change the face of the ground 'as nature has placed it'.

Sutherland pursued his case in every quarter. The lost bunker became the talking point of the day. It was certainly the talking point at a private dinner on 10 August 1869 given by publisher John Blackwood, who was then the tenant of Strathtyrum House, the estates of which adjoin the Links. The guests at the dinner included the cousins Sir Alexander Kinloch and Mr Robert Dalzell (both of whom were to become captains of the R&A), who agreed that the vandalism of the Green Committee was not to be allowed. So, after dinner, the cousins sallied forth in their evening clothes, roused the gardener, and persuaded him with the promise of gold to supply them with spades and a wheelbarrow and to give his help. They made their way to the Links, where they laboured all night, and by morning the bunker was restored. Before they left they wrote the name SUTHERLAND on a piece of paper, which they placed in a prominent place in the bunker and went off for a well-earned rest. Everyone thought it was Sutherland's work, and the bunker is known by the name Sutherland to this day.

The two adventurers finished their covert work at 4 a.m. They managed to keep their secret for many years, but their nocturnal and unaccustomed labours had played havoc with their pivot and their putting touch, and their sudden and simultaneous loss of form cost them a good half crown or two in their meetings with their golfing cronies.

Quite close to Sutherland but in the rough directly opposite Cottage bunker there was Hull's bunker. This left quite a narrow strip of fairway between the two bunkers, and it was felt that this was unfair, particularly when the course was standardised on the right-hand circuit. It then became very attractive to tee shots from the fifteenth. An attempt was made to close the bunker in 1920 when the R&A's Bunkers Committee put forward proposals for the creation of new bunkers – mostly on the outward half – and the closing of Hull's. But the general meeting on 4 May threw out the proposal, and Hull's bunker remained to torment players until the winter of 1949. The autumn general meeting approved the closure, but because the Links were, by that time, back in the ownership of the Town Council, their consent had to be obtained. This slight delay meant that the bunker was still available for its devious duty during the Dunlop Masters Tournament in October 1949.

Hull's took its name from the Revd Richard A. Hull, a son of R.P.B. Hull of Buxton in Derbyshire. He was ordained a clergyman of the

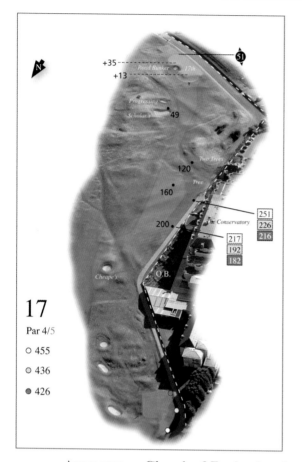

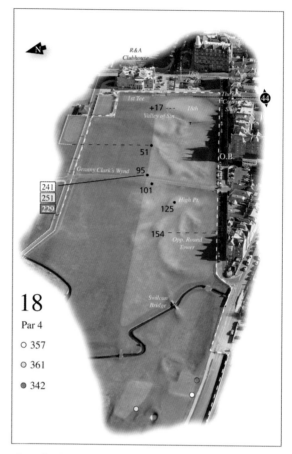

17

Par 4/5

○ 455

○ 436

● 426

18

Par 4

○ 357

○ 361

● 342

ABOVE LEFT:
The Road Hole

ABOVE RIGHT:
Tom Morris

Church of England and moved to St Andrews in 1878. He was a proficient golfer, who played frequently with the great Freddie Tait, and he won the R&A's Bombay Medal in 1886. But it was as a legislator in golf that he was best known. He was one of the original members of the club's Green Committee, set up after the passing of the 1894 Links Act, and served as its chairman from 1903 to 1912. He also gave distinguished service to the club's Rules of Golf Committee. He died in 1917 at the age of 73.

The Cottage bunker, which was the next door neighbour of Hull's, stretched across the fourth (now the 15th) fairway and took its name from Pilmour Cottage, which nestles in the spinney to the south.

The Student's bunkers used to be an important cluster of hazards guarding the old fourth green on the left-hand circuit but nowadays they come into play to trap a pulled second shot to the fourth green on the right-hand circuit. It is said they took their name from the practice of university students, short of time, playing only four holes out and four back.

The main hazard when playing from the old fifth tee was the famous Hell bunker; nowadays, negotiating the bunker forms an important part of the strategy in playing the 14th. It was, and still is to some extent, a terrifying

RIGHT: Hell bunker, the notorious hazard on the 14th fairway of the Old Course (Masakuni Akiyama)

110

bunker, although most golfers would agree that a visit to a large bunker is preferable to a session in a small 'pot', of which there are several forming satellites around Hell, such as the Devil's Kitchen and the Graves, so named because of their original coffin shapes.

The Beardies, still a formidable hazard to players driving from the 14th, had an almost magnetic attraction for balls on the old fifth, for the ground tends to slope towards them. The story goes that the Beardies were the home of gnomes, but it is difficult to believe that hard-headed Scots would place much credence in such a fairy tale. It is much more likely that the bunkers took their name from the long, spiky marram grasses which grew beard-like down the steep face of the hazards. Bunkers in those days were not manicured as they are today.

The Hole o' Cross bunker, which has almost disappeared, used to be a fearsome hazard when the hole was played as the fifth. The third stroke, assuming that the player had safely negotiated Hell and the Beardies, presented a nerve-shattering challenge across a chasm almost knee-deep in heather. The high-fronted Hole o' Cross bunker was set into the high mound protecting the green.

Driving from the old sixth tee, Mr James Walkinshaw, a delightful character whose enthusiasm for the game greatly exceeded his proficiency, invariably landed in a nasty little 'pot' set in the hillock about 100 yards from the tee. It is a tiny bunker, but almost as deep as it is wide. Whether or not fate was against Walkinshaw, it seemed that his ball always went into the bunker 'on the wrong side', for Walkinshaw was left-handed. The hazard became known as 'Walkinshaw's Grave' for 'he could not keep out of it, and he could not get out of it'. James Walkinshaw and his wife were well liked in St Andrews; they lived in a terraced house in Gillespie Terrace only a pitch and putt from the first tee.

Just beside Walkinshaw's Grave, cut into the side of the hill, is another nasty bunker known as the Cat's Trap, so called, it is believed, because it is unseen from the fairway and catches an unsuspecting ball, just as a cat ambushes a mouse.

We have skipped over the Lion's Mouth because it was of little moment to those playing the old sixth, but nowadays it traps many a ball which lands too short of the present 13th green. This bunker is often confused with the deep bunker which guards the right-hand corner of the 13th. This bunker boasts no name as yet, but it has been called a few in its time.

Nearer to the old sixth green is Nick's bunker, believed to be associated with Auld Nick, a Scotsman's term of endearment for the Devil.

Playing the old seventh, or High Hole, a bunker with a high facing bank had to be carried. If a drive was caught, it meant the certain loss of at least one stroke, and so it became known as Stroke bunker.

At the cross-over for the seventh and 11th holes there is a trio of bunkers. The first, guarding the left side of the present 11th green, is cut deeply into the side of a hill to merit the name Hill. Guarding the right-hand side of the green is Strath, one of the better-known St Andrews hazards. It is a permanent reminder of the Strath brothers, especially Davie, who in the early 1870s played frequently with Tommy Morris and was one of the few who could stand up to him on the golf course. The largest of the triumvirate of bunkers – that which guards the seventh green – is the Shell bunker, previously known as Cockle because of its base of cockle shells, now almost disappeared under successive layers of sand.

It will have been noted that the natural bunkers, those with the colourful names, are on the left-hand side of the course – the original circuit. Most of the bunkers on the outward holes as players know them today are man-made, strategically sited to replace the vast forest of whin which once covered the Links. Much of the clearance was undertaken by Old Tom Morris, who appears to have had a fairly free hand in his operations, although towards the end of the nineteenth century and the beginning of the twentieth, the Green Committee under J.L. Low was very active in planning the outgoing hazards.

Probably the last naming of bunkers took place at the beginning of the twentieth century, when Old Tom was carrying out improvements at the ninth. He created two bunkers about 100 yards from the ninth tee. The

How the notorious Hell bunker on the 14th hole used to be (St Andrews University)

The right-hand bunker guarding the approach to the 5th green (Masakuni Akiyama)

Boer War was being fought at the time, and great publicity surrounded the siege of Mafeking. Tom's workmen created an effigy of Paul Kruger, the obdurate president of the Transvaal, stuffed it with pitch and other flammable material, and held a ceremonial burning. It is related that it was at the suggestion of *Golf Illustrated* that the newly created bunkers should be called Kruger. The workmen made it a family affair by applying the name Mrs Kruger to a nearby hazard skulking in the heather, ready to catch a pulled drive from the ninth tee. A bunker near the left-hand corner of the ninth green used to be called Cronje, after the Boer leader who surrendered in 1900 following the relief of Kimberley, but the name seems to have disappeared from the course maps.

THE SWILCAN BURN

The Swilcan Burn, which cuts across the first and 18th fairways of the Old Course, has followed the same channel since 1880. At that time it formed the boundary between the property of Mr Cheape of Strathtyrum and the town's common. Until then it had meandered across the course in various channels determined by tide and flood, but towards the end of 1879 there were rumblings among local people that the course of the Swilcan was being deliberately altered. Whether deliberately or without forethought, Mr Cheape had been dumping waste material on his side of the Swilcan, with the result that the course of the burn changed, reclaiming ground on Mr Cheape's side and eroding the town's commonty. It was left to a member of the R&A to fight the local cause, and he was

Golfer and caddie successfully negotiate the burn and cross the bridge to the 18th fairway (Tina Norris)

quite forthright in his attack. On the night of 9 September 1879, Mr J.C. Fernie hired a large gang of labourers who worked non-stop through the night to restore the Swilcan to what he believed was its original course – the course at the time when Mr Cheape bought the Links from the Dempsters in 1821.

The sight of the restored Swilcan gladdened the local hearts but Mr Cheape was not amused, considering Mr Fernie's actions to be an invasion of his rights, and within a few days he had raised an action for damages against Mr Fernie. Mr Fernie sought the support of St Andrews Town Council in the action, claiming that the burn had been restored to its former course, that a decided improvement had been made and that 'not an inch of Mr Cheape's property has been taken'.

The Town Council did not take sides in the matter, and Mr Cheape's action in the Court of Session was successful. The court found that Mr Cheape was entitled to have the course of the burn restored, and Mr Fernie was ordered to pay the cost of the action and the damages. Mr Fernie apologised, and Mr Cheape accepted his apology – and the £30 which he offered as expenses. Mr Cheape, on his part, agreed that the course of the Swilcan should remain.

The course of the Swilcan Burn is now fixed

CHANGING FACILITIES

The provision of clubhouse or changing facilities for visiting golfers has always been a problem at St Andrews, and many unkind words were hurled in the past at St Andrews Town Council and the Links Trust for their failure to find a solution to it.

The problem is worth examining in depth. The location of the courses, particularly the Old Course, is the seat of the problem. If they are not bounded by the sea, they are hemmed in by other buildings. The difficulty is exacerbated by the change in holiday habits since the Second World War. There was a time when the golfing holidaymaker booked into a hotel or boarding house with his wife and family and stayed for a week, a fortnight or even longer. The hotel or boarding house was their clubhouse and no problems were apparent.

Casual, one-off golfers were few but their requirements were met through an unwritten understanding between the local golf clubs and the Town Council which arose from the 1913 Links Act. The Town Council was empowered to issue concession tickets to club members who were not resident in St Andrews, and this brought a sudden and unexpected prosperity to the clubs through greatly increased 'country memberships'. In gratitude for this concession, the clubs opened their doors to casual visitors, either by their being 'signed in' or vouched for by a member or by offering temporary membership at very modest rates. The clubs usually set aside a small number of lockers for this purpose, and it was a service which the golfer appreciated as an act of hospitality and which the clubs welcomed as an additional money-spinner.

But by the 1960s these leisurely holiday habits changed, air travel had brought St Andrews closer to the United States, Europe and Japan, and the popularity of the game had flourished worldwide, mainly through the medium of television.

Golfers all over the world regarded St Andrews as the Mecca of the game – or the 'Home of Golf' – and a visit to St Andrews became something of a pilgrimage. The pilgrims, though, were golfers in a hurry, anxious to cram in as many venues as their itinerary permitted – Turnberry, Gleneagles, Carnoustie and, if they had friends at court, Muirfield, and the great English courses such as Lytham, Birkdale, Hoylake and Wentworth. Many of the pilgrims came on package tours organised through tourist agencies, and, while they may, in aggregate, have brought something to the tourist trade, they could in no way have been regarded as a boon to the local holiday caterers. Usually they came in busloads organised from some distant hotel base, provided with packed lunches and already dressed for golf. All they had to do before walking onto the course was to change their shoes.

St Andrews Town Council addressed itself to the problem over many years. The first attempt at a solution was made just after the Second World War, when the council took the former Bay Tea Room building, which stood on the site now occupied by the British Golf Museum. But at one end of the old building there was a public toilet, which was by no stretch of the imagination a pleasant one, and few people were able to forget it, even when the toilets were upgraded to form part of the changing-rooms. The atmosphere was not improved by the fitting of steel doors, which clanged behind the patrons, earning it the nickname Sing-Sing. The male patrons, single-minded in their attitude to golf, did not complain too bitterly, but the ladies did not like it. They expected something more comfortable, even sumptuous.

The pavilion on the 'old' Eden Course – the first golf changing-rooms in St Andrews erected by the Town Council after the purchase of the course in 1936 (St Andrews University)

The Eden Course had its own pavilion, built shortly after the council purchased the course. There were lockers, toilets and showers but no catering facilities. When tournaments were in progress on the Eden, self-service catering machines were brought in.

The Joint Links Committee considered the problem at the New and Jubilee courses, and, since the first tees were only a few yards apart, it was considered that one pavilion would meet the needs of both courses. Fred Hawtree of Addington was brought in to advise the committee, and he offered suggestions which involved resiting the first tee and the 18th green of the Jubilee and extending the car park. The work was started in 1966 and was completed at a cost of just over £12,000. It housed office accommodation for the starter, storage for caddie carts, toilets and showers.

But the problem affecting the Old Course would not go away. The town clerk, Mr Neil Mackenzie, made an analysis of the situation, and his exhaustive report concluded:

> The general conclusion seems to be that the number of players who would make use of the accommodation is very limited, but that the lack of such accommodation is a genuine difficulty for some. This applies particularly to women, who tend to expect attractive surroundings comparable to a clubhouse or a hotel. It also appears that parking space in the immediate vicinity is a sine qua non. This raises again the question of parking space in the vicinity of the start of the Old Course. There is, of course, only one place – the east end of the Bruce Embankment – and if this is not acceptable, the problem must be written off as insoluble.

The council looked at other possibilities – the premises of Robert Forgan and Sons overlooking the 18th green – but the problem again was parking space.

Parking space was provided at the east end of the Bruce Embankment in 1969. It was just about this time that proposals were brought out for a reorganisation of local government in Scotland, and the unspoken thought in every councillor's mind was 'If we are to embark on heavy capital expenditure, let's do it now, so that the burden of repayment and maintenance will fall on a broader-based local authority.' So the Town Council pursued the project with renewed vigour.

By 1971, plans were drawn up for a pavilion on the Bruce Embankment. It was to have changing-rooms, a golf museum and catering facilities, but the R&A, who had been consulted about the plans from the start, objected when they realised that the building line of the pavilion would be 25 feet farther west than the west frontage of their clubhouse and this would impair the view from the 'Big Room'. The council offered to take it ten feet back, but the club was adamant and threatened to protest to the Secretary of State for Scotland. The Town Council was reluctant to move the site farther east because it would reduce the space available for parking. There were objections from other parties and the proposal was shelved.

A suggestion was made that the pavilion should be built on the greensward behind the 18th green. The site had been proposed some years earlier, but had been turned down because it would be 'a blot on the skyline', but the planning officer believed that if the ground was excavated the building would 'sit down'. However, the plan was plagued by protests led by the directors of the then Golf Hotel. Time was running short, and the Town Council decided to ask for plans on a less ambitious scale, using the site of the existing changing-rooms – the old Bay Tea Room – with Golf Place being rerouted straight across the Bruce Embankment putting-green. The burgh chamberlain then dropped a financial bombshell on the council by reporting that domestic rates would rise by seven pence in the pound and on commercial premises by ten pence in the pound. This left the council with a bad attack of financial nerves, so instead of demolishing the Bay Tea Room they decided to do a little exterior alteration, provide new entrances and completely reorganise the interior. There would be a large waiting room with timber-clad walls and a telephone connection with the Old Course starter. The plans had to be approved by the Secretary of State for Scotland, which caused a delay of six months, bringing the council dangerously close to the date of reorganisation. But it also gave the councillors time to reflect that they had made no provision for office accommodation for the Links Trust and Management Committee. The plans were redrawn, allowing for cloakrooms and office accommodation. The Town Council approved the plans, leaving themselves in the old position, with no pavilion and changing-rooms reduced to cloakrooms on the same site with the same unsavoury atmosphere. But no one could say that the Town Council hadn't tried.

The Town Council's problem became a problem for the Links Trust in 1974. How did they tackle it?

They felt that if it was not possible to have a purpose-built clubhouse on new ground, they must acquire property and adapt it to their needs. In 1980, the Trust made approaches to the management of Rusack's Hotel overlooking the 18th fairway of the Old Course. They wanted to lease or purchase the lower ground floor but they were unsuccessful. In the following year, they made a successful bid for the whole hotel. The Trustees had become reluctant hotel-keepers, and this raised problems about their charitable status. They overcame this difficulty by forming a limited liability company, to which they rented the major part of the hotel, leaving the lower ground floor to be developed as changing-rooms, bar and so on under the direct control of the Trust.

While the acquisition of the hotel went a long way to meeting the catering needs of visiting golfers, it had one major disadvantage. Car parking space at the hotel was limited, and, while there was ample space available in a rather rudimentary car park behind the 17th green, it fell short of the 'car-to-door' service which the Trust had aimed for and which the visiting golfer seemed to expect. The rooms were officially opened on 20 July 1983.

The catering services proved to be popular with local people and the hotel residents, but the locker-rooms, changing facilities and showers were little used, and it was something of a disappointment that the new development did not seem to be attracting the type of golfing patronage that the Trust had targeted. In addition, the Trustees were very sensitive about their relationship with the local catering industry.

The Trust's affair with the hotel business was a short one, for in July 1985 they sold the hotel with all its fittings to Trust House Forte plc, who undertook to use the lower ground floor as Links Rooms with lockers and showers. While the transaction relieved the Trust of its uneasy status as hotelier, it put the real problem of changing accommodation back on the drawing board.

St Andrews
Links Clubhouse

The Trust then looked at the possibility of erecting a multi-purpose building on land occupied by the Ladies' Putting Club (the Himalayas). It was to house the whole of the Links administration and provide accommodation for caddies and changing facilities for golfers using the Old, New and Jubilee courses, along with bar and catering facilities.

The general public of St Andrews did not like it and expressed its views at a public meeting called by the Trustees in 1988. The residents did not like the look of the building, which they claimed obscured the view to the north. They felt it was out of sympathy with the natural character of the Links, and they took the view that the building was so far from each of the three courses that it would serve none of them adequately. After hearing these views, the Trust agreed to have another look at the problem.

After considering a variety of sites and options, the Trustees came up with a new proposal which received planning consent at the beginning of 1993. The new building was planned to have male and female locker-rooms, lounge, bar and dining room and a reception concourse. The site was roughly that of the former starter's office and changing-rooms which served the New and Jubilee courses, but it covered an area of 15,000 square feet. It had the advantage of being next to an existing, large car park.

The Links Clubhouse was designed to sit low in its surroundings

Golfers intending to play the Old Course would be conveyed to the first tee by a 'buggy' service operating along a specially strengthened lane. The whole work, which cost £3 million, did not command universal approval when the plans were first made public, but the Trustees had, through their architects, the Hurd Rolland Partnership, arranged to contour the two-storey building into its natural surroundings so that it had the appearance of a single-storey building when seen from the east. A roof terrace was incorporated, as well as a balcony at the entrance level, giving panoramic views of the courses and back into the town. Despite many local misgivings, the Links Clubhouse became a considerable success after only its first year, attracting both townspeople and visitors through its doors. After almost 50 years of trying, there were clubhouse facilities freely available to all golfers on the Links.

While the Links Clubhouse met the needs of golfers using the testing circuits of the Old, New and Jubilee courses, children, elderly people, learners and casual golfers using the less demanding Eden, Strathtyrum and Balgove courses and the practice area had very few facilities.

Built in 1995 amid much controversy, the Links Clubhouse overlooks the 1st tee and the 18th green of the New Course

Pilmour Cottage, *c.*1910, was originally the Dower House for Strathtyrum Estate. It was acquired by the Links Trust in 1989 from the Old Course Hotel, which had been using it for staff accommodation

There was also a problem left over resulting from the construction of the Links Clubhouse. The reduction in its size as a concession to local objectors meant that the Trust's administrative operations continued to be housed partly in the decaying 160-year-old Pilmour Cottage and partly in temporary Portakabins. Trustees decided to kill two birds with one stone by developing Pilmour Cottage to provide both clubhouse facilities for golfers on the west side of the Links and more satisfactory office space for the administration. The building was extended at the back and on both sides creating a two-storey building to accommodate a new clubhouse and the offices in a single unit. The clubhouse took up all of the ground floor, and the upper floor accommodated the offices.

Costing £1.3 million, the new complex was designed by architect Fraser Smart and constructed to a high standard, similar in style to its senior, the Links Clubhouse, with large windows and wood finishes generating an atmosphere of space and warmth. The lounge and bar are open to everyone year round and command a discreet view of the first tee of the Eden Course. For those with scenic rather than critical interests, a short spiralling stair led to the upper floor, but this space was later used for offices.

The locker-rooms were equipped to satisfy the most fastidious of golfers with showers, hairdryers, clothes-drying facilities, overnight storage for clubs and shoes, and ultrasonic club cleaning – and there is even a gadget for changing from metal to plastic shoe spikes.

Recognising the need to encourage youngsters in golf, the Trust made provision for a special room for Juniors to meet in casual informality for refreshment or to await collection by family or friends.

The complex was opened in April 2000 by Menzies Campbell, MP for North East Fife, who was at the time a Links Trustee. In view of its considerable enlargement and proximity to the newly purchased Pilmour Lodge, it was felt that the name should be changed from Pilmour Cottage to Pilmour House.

When the seventh course – later to become The Castle Course – was being planned, a clubhouse was an integral part of the project from the start. It was felt that the clubhouse would have to be spectacular and of a standard that would match the course and the setting. However, it was only allowed to be single storey, and effectively invisible from the town, to meet the stipulations of Fife Council's planning committee. This constraint had been imposed as a result of the furore surrounding the building of the St Andrews Bay hotel and the associated clubhouse on the town's skyline three years earlier. These developments were considered to be all too visible from the town's historic area, and the councillors wanted no repeat of the trouble caused.

Opened in 2000, the Eden Clubhouse can provide refreshments al fresco in good weather

Fraser Smart, the architect, suggested a circular single-storey building with huge plate glass windows in the lounge, giving magnificent panoramic views of the town, the 9th and 18th greens, and over the bay to Carnoustie and the mountains. It was to be built in Caithness stone and have a copper roof. After checking the cost implications, the Trustees agreed. Built beside the site of the mediaeval Kinkell Castle, of which no trace remained, the clubhouse reception area displays an oil painting based on an eighteenth-century drawing of the castle and its setting. One unusual feature of the clubhouse is its heating and cooling mechanism, which uses the environmentally friendly ground source heat pump system. Expensive to install but economical to run, it was calculated that the capital cost would be recouped in less than ten years.

The building's circularity, however, did cause a number of design and construction headaches, with the result that completion was delayed to within a whisker of the official opening of the course.

The Links had gone from having no clubhouses at all to having three excellent facilities in the space of thirteen years.

The clubhouse at
The Castle Course
(Russell Kirk)

PRACTICE MAKES PERFECT

In earlier times, practising was done on the course itself, and as the Old Course was very close to the town, it was especially convenient to practise on what are now the first and 18th holes. As the popularity of the game increased, however, this became increasingly impractical, not to say dangerous.

There was no specific practice ground until after the opening of the Eden Course, when the field on the other side of the wall at the 17th hole came into use. Its length, however, was not sufficient to provide driving practice.

In the 1930s a private company, St Andrews Golf School Ltd, operated a teaching school and driving range on university land on the North Haugh, only a pitch and putt from the start of the Eden Course. After the Second World War, the school and range were taken over by J.D. (Jock) McAndrew, who had spent most of his professional life teaching golf in Argentina. On Jock's death, the business was carried on by his brother Bert, an accountant and one-time professional golfer. When the university required the use of the land for the expansion of its science departments, the range was contracted and ultimately disappeared. The loss of the range was sorely felt by visitors and by the locals.

In August 1965, the Town Council asked their Links supervisor for his views on the provision of a driving range, and he told the Town Council that the only site which appeared to be available was at the far end of the Jubilee Course. The area required was 300 yards by 200 yards – about 12½ acres – and the essential requirements were accessibility, reasonably level ground, safety and the least possible disturbance of the existing layout. These conditions, he felt, could be provided by using parts of the ninth, tenth, 11th and 12th fairways of the Jubilee Course, but alternative holes would have to be constructed. He offered as an alternative an area near the 13th green of the Jubilee Course, but he added that this would involve some reconstruction, and even then there would be an undulating surface.

The Town Council decided that both sites were too far from the centre of the golfing activity to commend themselves for development as a driving range.

The quest was ended when in 1989–90 the Links Trust put into action the plan which removed the first, second, 17th and 18th fairways from the Eden Course. The intention was that the ground should be used for establishing a driving range and practice area which could be diverted for housing the tented village at Open Championships. Work was completed in 1993 when the £300,000 Golf Practice Centre was opened by the British Ladies' Champion, Catriona Lambert.

The new range proved to be one of the most popular of the new additions to the golfing complex. After only seven-and-a-half months, most of that spanning the winter months, 50,000 buckets of balls had been smacked down the range, and by the end of its first year 100,000 buckets had blazed their distinctive trails through rain, hail and sunshine.

So successful were the new practice facilities that within a dozen years plans were being drawn up to increase the number of bays in the driving range and to introduce additional services.

It was felt that not only were more covered bays required but also that a modern golf teaching facility should be provided along with a club-fitting operation, to keep at the forefront of golfing development. These last two activities were, the Trustees decided, to be franchised out. The Golf Academy was to be operated by PGA Golf Management, and the club fitting by a local man, Ed Robertson, who was rapidly developing a good reputation in this field.

A specification for the extension was drawn up and detailed plans prepared by Fraser Smart, the architect responsible for the design of the original range.

The driving range with the new bays of the extension at the far end

Some hiccups in the construction process delayed the opening, but in June 2006 the public were allowed in to try out the new facilities. Any doubts were soon dispelled: the extension and the new services were up to the mark. An official opening by Peter Dawson, the Chief Executive of the R&A, followed a few weeks later.

As well as doubling the number of covered bays, the extension housed four specialist bays for teaching

Peter Dawson, Chief Executive of the R&A, declares the extended driving range open

and club fitting, all of which were packed with the latest technology. The advances that had taken place in coaching aids in the 13 years since the Golf Practice Centre first opened were of a complexity unimaginable in 1993 – and even more so in the days of the crude 150-yard-long practice field which existed before that.

The new Academy's coaching service proved popular, and Ed Robertson's club-fitting service was used by golfers from all over Scotland. The new bays were in constant use and the original ones were as busy as ever.

Golf Academy Director of Instruction Steve North helps a young golfer get to grips with the swing

THE BRUCE EMBANKMENT

One of the greatest reclamation exercises ever undertaken in St Andrews resulted in the creation of the greensward which lies between the first fairway of the Old Course and the West Sands. The project was an extension of the reclamation scheme undertaken on the first and 18th fairways by Provost Sir Hugh Lyon Playfair to combat the erosive action of high tides on these fairways.

In 1893, Mr George Bruce, a prominent St Andrews citizen and member of the Town Council, helped by his architect son, George Bruce Jr, devised a plan for reclaiming additional land. At the same time, the town's sewer outfall, which was disagreeably close to the R&A Clubhouse and the rapidly developing holiday beaches, could be extended. The basis of Bruce's idea was to place four old fishing boats roughly north to south at the east end of the reclamation area. Members of the Town Council and of the general public poured scorn and ridicule upon it, but the Bruces were confident and went ahead with the scheme at their own expense. They bought the four old boats that they needed in St Andrews Harbour and towed them the half mile or so to the embankment. With the help of the fishermen, they placed the boats in position, chained them bow to stern and, after pouring concrete into the hulls, they filled them up with heavy stones. It was hard, back-breaking work: the stones had to be moved manually, and old Bruce, a powerfully built man, took his full share in the frustrating task – frustrating because, time after time, heavy seas and high tides lifted the landlocked craft out of position, and they had to be reset.

In the course of time, the sea and the weather gave them sufficient respite to complete a sloping barricade on the east side of the boats by driving stakes into the foreshore. By this time, the Town Council was beginning to appreciate the practicality of George Bruce's dream, and they did not need much persuasion to help the process of reclamation by using the area westwards of the boat barricade as a dump for the town's refuse. This brought with it temporary problems, for while the refuse was being dumped, the area was invaded by rats, which from time to time intruded into the R&A Clubhouse in search of a taste of gracious living. The club appears to have accepted the embankment as a means, ultimately, of protecting their clubhouse and the course, and they made no great issue of having to engage their own Pied Piper to get rid of the rats. Later, the Town Council erected

a concrete wall along the north face of the embankment and continued it as a concrete breakwater to join up with the Doo Craig (or Dhu Craig, as some would have it).

The creation of the Bruce Embankment brought some problems – not serious, but sufficient to warrant a petition to the Town Council in 1896 for a proper name to be given to the area which, until then, was known as the Boat Embankment. But the question of the name was really a front for raising the larger issue of whether the embankment should form part of the Links.

Mr William Brown, who sponsored the petition, made no secret of his feelings that the embankment should not form part of the Links; it had sometimes been referred to as the Links Embankment, and he found this objectionable. It could be used for purposes other than golf, and it provided an excellent route to the West Sands without crossing the Links. He wanted it to be known as the Bruce Embankment, which he felt would be a compliment to a thoroughly popular and deserving citizen. But Bailie John Milne, a confirmed royalist who had designed the Victoria Memorial Arch at Fettercairn, wanted it to be known as the Queen's Embankment. His motion failed to find a seconder, and he was the only dissenter from 'the Bruce Embankment'.

Early work on the reclamation of the Bruce Embankment in 1893. Four old fishing boats are in position to form the basis of the eastern bulwark of the embankment, and cartloads of stone are being dumped into the hulls. In the background is Doo Craig rock, which was later linked to the embankment by a concrete breakwater (St Andrews University)

The Town Council, at a meeting on 6 June 1904, took an important decision on the future of the Bruce Embankment when it was resolved 'in view of the large expenditure of money on the Bruce Embankment' that the footpath from the north-east corner of the R&A Clubhouse to the Swilcan Burn, and all the ground to the north thereof, would be reserved for the purpose of walking and 'that golf should not be played thereon'.

Several proposals were made for the development of the embankment, a strong favourite being tennis courts, but the site was rejected after much argument about its exposed position. The same reasons were used against its development as a bowling green, and eventually, in 1914, the Town Council agreed, despite the 1904 resolution, that it should be laid out as a public putting course, that being an activity complementary to golf. It was used from time to time as the tented village at major golfing events, but as the commercial potential of the village was exploited, the Championship Committee started to look for bigger sites. The embankment is still used to accommodate hospitality tents and the press centre on big occasions.

The Bruce
Embankment
putting green
in 2008

CHANGES FOR CROWD CONTROL

The 1932 Links Act empowered the Town Council to charge spectators for viewing during major golfing events, its purpose being to keep the crowds down to manageable proportions. In the early days of gate money, no special control arrangements were involved beyond a steward and a team of helpers with ropes. But crowds continued to increase, and it was found necessary to confine spectators to the sidelines and keep them off the playing areas.

The layout of the St Andrews courses meant that changes there would have to be more severe than at any other championship venue if paying customers were to get value for money. It was perhaps the beginning of the commercialisation of golf; a small beginning perhaps, but it did a great deal to change the character of the Old Course.

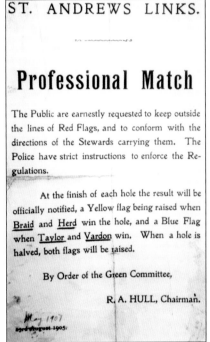

ST. ANDREWS LINKS.

Professional Match

The Public are earnestly requested to keep outside the lines of Red Flags, and to conform with the directions of the Stewards carrying them. The Police have strict instructions to enforce the Regulations.

At the finish of each hole the result will be officially notified, a Yellow flag being raised when Braid and Herd win the hole, and a Blue Flag when Taylor and Vardon win. When a hole is halved, both flags will be raised.

By Order of the Green Committee,

R. A. HULL, Chairman.

This notice shows how crowds were regulated and how the results were indicated to them during the playing of big-money professional matches in 1907

The Old Course was skirted by dense walls of whin bushes, which placed a high premium on straight driving, and this was why 'keep left' was the advice given to newcomers. Indeed, until the early 1930s there was no other way to go. But with spectators being banned from the playing area, these masses of whin and gorse formed a screen between spectators and play, and drastic measures were necessary. During the later 1930s, and continuing through the years of the Second World War with the help of prisoners of war, masses of gorse were cleared from the fringes of the Old Course, particularly at the outgoing holes, so that spectators would have some sort of viewing facility. This had the side effect of opening up the course, and, while it was still accepted that it was 'safer down the left', the bolder and more accurate drivers were willing to take a chance down the right with the rewarding prospect of an easier shot to the green.

OVERLEAF: The 'March of the Alcan golfers' through the town to the Old Course provided a ceremonial start to the inaugural Alcan Tournament in October 1967 (D.C. Thomson)

As more and more spectators flocked to St Andrews, other means of providing viewing facilities had to be found. A huge artificial mound was constructed near the sixth tee, and in 1964, in preparation for the Open Championship which came to be known as 'Tony Lema's', other viewing mounds were built overlooking the second, fifth, 13th and 17th greens, and an extra special one was positioned behind the 14th tee, giving a spectacular view down the fairway lane between the Beardies and the out-of-bounds wall of the Eden Course. Viewing mounds were also provided behind the third and fourth tees and a raised walk was formed to the right of the sixth fairway. All this involved some adjustment of teeing areas, which resulted in a reduction of the overall length of the championship course by ten yards – from 6,936 to 6,926. The outward nine were actually increased by 38 yards, but the inward nine were shortened by 48 yards.

Wildlife enthusiasts and nature conservationists were not so numerous nor so vocal in those days, and the controversy which all this would have sparked off had it happened in the present day can well be imagined.

Crowds scamper over the fairways and through bunkers before effective control confined them to the sidelines (G.M. Cowie)

SUNDAY GOLF

Sunday golf has never been permitted, in the ordinary run of things, over the Old Course, but exceptions are made for important golfing events and for filming. The course is public, and, unlike most championship courses, it takes a tremendous pounding. Tom Morris's dictum was 'If the gowfer disna need a rest, the course does', and management has always been careful to nurture this jewel in its golfing crown. Intervals between starting times have been extended from four minutes in the 1920s and '30s to eight minutes in the 1980s and to ten minutes in 1990. The course also used to have a month's rest each year for repair and recovery, but early in the twenty-first century this was replaced with 'maintenance Mondays', days in the winter months when the course was closed. A further protective measure was the introduction of fairway mats – small, portable rectangles of plastic grass on which the golfers placed their golf balls when playing from the fairways in winter. This measure was estimated to save the course from having around 150,000 divot holes scarring the fairways as a result of winter play. Despite all these additional protective measures, there is still no Sunday play.

But on the other St Andrews courses things are different. Changing attitudes to Sunday observance and the advantages, both commercial and recreational, of opening the courses have been acknowledged. In a place like St Andrews, which was the centre of the Reformation in Scotland, it was probably only to be expected that change would be slower than elsewhere. It was the Second World War which broke the religious ice. The town had become a wartime centre for military training, and every available inch of accommodation was requisitioned for young soldiers and airmen. The clubhouse of the New Golf Club was taken over as living accommodation, and, in addition to this massive new influx of young servicemen and women, there was a huge increase in personnel at RAF Leuchars, about five miles away.

All this youthful energy needed a recreational outlet, and the Town Council decided in 1941 that the Eden Course only should be open for play on Sundays after 1 p.m., but in making this decision they agreed that on the cessation of hostilities a plebiscite of the St Andrews residents should be taken to discover whether they wished Sunday golf on the Eden to be a permanent feature.

The substantive decision to open the Eden Course on Sundays was taken at a special meeting of the Town Council on 19 June 1941, held to regularise a decision taken on 2 June which people felt had contravened the council's Standing Orders. Some members of the council wanted a plebiscite to be taken there and then, but it was argued that so many of the locals were absent on wartime service and so many servicemen were in training in the town that a plebiscite taken at that time would not be a true reflection of St Andrews opinion. The proposal was narrowly rejected by six votes to five.

It was a time, perhaps, when St Andreans reflected on the wickedness of two sons of Alexander Miller, who in 1583 were rash enough to wield a golf club on the 'golf fields' on the Sabbath, and who accordingly incurred the wrath of the Kirk Session whose Ordinances they had breached. Nevertheless, on Sunday, 29 June 1941, two airmen, Cadets Parkinson and Tulip, struck the first legalised Sunday golf shots from the first tee of the Eden Course. Among the spectators who witnessed the inauguration was Mr W.J. Rusack, who had driven the first ball after the course was officially opened in 1914 by Mrs Herkless.

The people of St Andrews trod timidly down this newly opened path to fire and brimstone, and even after ten months of Sunday play, the drawings for the day, 15 March 1942, totalled only £1 18s, made up of two visitors at 3s each, twenty members of the Forces at 1s 6d each and two cars parked for 1s each. In addition, 16 residents played without charge, since the Links Acts, up to then, had vested no power in the Town Council to charge local people for golf.

But as more and more people became used to the idea, more of them risked the fires of hell which lay ahead, and by 9 April – only four weeks later – the takings had doubled to £3 16s with nine visitors, twenty-eight members of the Forces and seven cars. But the canny residents had faded slightly to 13.

True to their word, the Town Council took a plebiscite of the local people in December 1945, despite protests from the Lord's Day Observance Society. The electors were asked whether they were in favour of Sunday golf being played on the Eden Course after 1 p.m. The result was: 2,412 in favour; 1,085 against – a majority of 1,327 in favour. At the same time, the council fixed the charge for visitors at 4s per round (double the weekday charge).

Things moved quickly after the ice had been broken, with the New and Jubilee courses opening for Sunday play and the restriction on the hours during which play was permitted being abolished. Only the Old Course remained untouchable for normal Sunday play, but it is used on Sundays from time to time for special events.

When the 1946 Links Act came into force, giving the Town Council power to charge local people for golf, Sunday golf was kept as a separate item and excluded from the coverage provided by the annual concession fee. A separate charge was made per round for Sunday play. But, in doing this, the council observed the unwritten law that the charge for residents should not exceed 25 per cent of that levied against other classes of golfer. It was not until the passage of the 1974 Act that the locals' charge for Sunday golf was included in the yearly ticket.

The town from the 15th green of the Old Course

THE LINKS ROAD WAR

The construction of Links Road, which forms the southern boundary of the 18th fairway of the Old Course, provoked scenes even more remarkable than those which accompanied the Rabbit Wars.

The 'Roads Case' reached its climax in February 1880, but its origins go back farther than that – to around 1820, when the Town Council sold plots of land between Pilmour Links and the golf course for building purposes. Houses were eventually built on these plots, but the owners had built right out to the limits of their ground, leaving themselves with no access to their houses except by way of the golf course. They stepped out of their houses directly onto part of the golfing area of the Links. Theoretically, this should have been in grass, but over weeks, months and years it had become a quagmire, rutted by the wheels of coaches and carts.

In May 1874, the house owners petitioned the Town Council for consent to lay down a road 21 feet wide from Golf Place to Granny Clark's Wynd, at their own expense. The estimated cost was £61 10s, and it was to include the erection of a line of posts with a chain to form a boundary between the golf course and the road. On this matter, the Town Council was split right down the middle. Some took the view that the Links were not only for golfers but for the whole community, of which the house owners formed part, and that the road was essential not only for the owners but for others going, for example, to and from the railway station, which at that time was situated on the area now occupied by the Old Course Hotel. Others took the view that the area proposed for the road was part of the golfing area and could not be set aside for any other purpose – even by the Town Council; they also expressed concern that the owners, having paid for the road, would consider it to be their property. A decision was reached in 1879 by the casting vote of the provost that the road should be laid down at the expense of the house owners.

Opponents of the road petitioned the court for interdict against the Town Council, but Lord Curriehill, the Lord Justice Ordinary, found that the pursuers had failed to make out any case for an interdict against the formation of a road and found them liable for expenses. At the same time, he sounded a warning to the Town Council:

The rights of the public in a place like St Andrews are of a sacred description and must not lightly be interfered with, and the magistrates must not suppose that they might go and make roads wherever they liked across the links and thereby interfere with the rights of the public. They must exercise due protection over the rights of all classes of the community.

There were some who wished to golf; there were others who simply wished to walk, and others to have a pleasant drive. If it was possible to adapt the Links to the use of all these classes so that each should have a fair share of the enjoyment of them, he thought the magistrates were quite entitled to do so. Unless it could be made very clear to the court that they were exceeding their discretion to a very serious extent, the court would be very slow indeed to interfere with the management. Therefore, he thought, on the whole matter, that the pursuers had failed to make out any case for an interdict against the formation of the road.

But litigants in St Andrews, in those days, were not easily discouraged, and if Fifers ever deserved the tag of being hard headed, it must have been earned in this case, for they appealed to the Court of Session, where the proceedings were heard in 1880 by the Lord Justice Clerk, along with Lords Ormidale and Gifford. The court upheld the decision of the Lord Ordinary, the Lord Justice Clerk adding a directive about the ownership of the road, stating that the magistrates and town councillors could not devolve either the property of the proposed road or the administration of it in any way on any third party and that it must remain in their own hands under their own control as the property of the burgh for the benefit of the community of the burgh.

Lords Ormidale and Gifford concurred in this and added their own views, which were recalled much later, in 1923, by Mr David Balsillie when the Town Council was about to sell a small pocket of land to the R&A for an extension to the clubhouse. Mr Balsillie's recollection caused the Town Council to realise that they had no power to alienate any of the common land, and they then had to seek this power through the 1924 Links Act.

The objectors still did not give up, and they intimated that they would appeal to the House of Lords. However, because of parliamentary holidays, there was some delay in lodging the appeal and the Town Council went ahead to construct the road.

On Saturday, 31 January 1880, the Town Council started to have the road levelled from the corner of Golf Place to the Swilcan Burn, and bottoming and road metal were laid down by a large squad of labourers, but the resumption of work on Monday was the signal for the battle to commence. Opponents of the road had assembled a strong gang of labourers, or 'navvies' as they were known, and a backup team of four carts. With unusual speed, they started to remove the bottoming and road metal which had been laid, and as quickly as the road-makers relaid it, they shovelled it away. The townspeople got to hear of the battle, and large crowds gathered to watch the fun. The town councillors appealed to the police, who had turned out in large numbers, but they refused to intervene, saying that they could only do so 'if there was a breach of the peace'.

Time after time, the road-makers laid down the road metal but it was immediately pounced upon and carted away. Two members of the Town Council stepped in – personally and literally – to try to stop the rot. Determined to prevent the removal of the metal, they stood on it as it was laid, but this was of no avail for the material was shovelled away from under their feet. This caused tempers to rise but fortunately no injuries were caused. The town seemed to be fighting a losing battle, but there was still a war to be won. The councillors on the spot held a council of war to discuss strategy and tactics. They conjectured, correctly, that the opposition forces were mercenaries with no interest in whether the road was built or not. The councillors offered more money than the objectors, so the opposition navvies switched sides to join the road-making forces. Within minutes, the two squads were working amicably side by side, bringing back the road metal and laying it in place. Of course, the Town Council also had to raise the rate of pay for their own loyal forces, and ultimately the going rate reached a staggering £1 per day – more than a man would earn normally in a week.

The opposition had been outmanoeuvred, but they wanted to fight on. They tried to engage more men and more carts in St Andrews, but none was available or willing. They dispatched a messenger to the rural village of Strathkinness about four miles away with authority to engage all available labourers and carts at any cost. But whether because of the excitement of the occasion, a copious hipflask or the operations of a 'fifth column', by the time the messenger reached Strathkinness he was, in the words of one observer, 'oblivious to all earthly things'. He was quite incapable to delivering his message, so he was driven back to St Andrews and quietly put to bed.

The opposition knew nothing of this, and while they waited for the navvies and the carts from Strathkinness their envoy was slumbering away, peacefully and snugly at home. But the opposition was not beaten yet; word reached the council that a squad of Irish labourers based at Dundee was on its way to St Andrews to join the opposition forces. The council's intelligence was reliable, and an agent was sent to Guardbridge to intercept them. Posing as one of the opposition, he told the squad that it was too late and their services were no longer required, and they returned to Dundee.

Meanwhile, a number of wheelbarrows were brought to the scene by the opposition, but they were soon hijacked. Then reinforcements arrived, supported by two carts. The Town Council had bargained with their own squad not only to put the metal down but to make sure that it remained down. The battle then erupted. Carts parted company with their wheels and spades and shovels were wielded freely if not effectively, for by this time darkness had fallen and oil lamps were not the ideal illumination for a pitched battle. So, although the clash of spade upon spade echoed across the Links, little damage was done to life or limb. The opposition was heavily outnumbered and the council's squad scored a notable victory. The remainder of the night passed off peacefully, perhaps because of the hospitality provided by the councillors. One member of the Town Council, who was opposed to the construction of the road, describing the 'disgraceful scenes' counted 53 men 'mortal drunk' – made so by the Road Committee.

The following morning dawned peacefully, if a little painfully for at least 53 of the combatants, and work on the road proceeded. Local people again turned out in large numbers to cheer or jeer. Many shopkeepers shut up shop for the day, and they were not disappointed. Rumour spread that a large squad of workers had been assembled at Strathkinness, and by two o'clock they had been marshalled in battle order, along with two carts in City Road. It seemed that battle was to be joined again, but the Town Council had petitioned for an interdict against the opposition. This was granted, and the Procurator Fiscal along with Captain George Bremner, Chief Constable of Fife, arrived on the scene. Captain Bremner intimated to the opposing forces that any interference with the construction of the road would lead to the apprehension of offenders, who would be jailed. The Strathkinness carts and the labour force withdrew quite happily after successful negotiations about pay.

By some clerical error, the interdict had not included that part of the road between Granny Clark's Wynd and the Swilcan Burn, and the local residents expected a resumption of the hostilities next day. A large police force had been assembled but it appeared that the opposition had had enough, for there was no further aggression.

Like all wars, it had been a costly affair. The feuars, or householders, had subscribed the money for the road, and with the high wages paid, it had all gone. It had been their intention to form a proper kerb and channel, but there was no money left. And 129 years later, there was still no proper kerb or channel in Links Road. It was March 1914 before the Town Council erected a fence alongside Links Road at a cost of £42 10s, and three months later before they painted it white – and white it is to this day.

IRRIGATION

The Links has had a gravitational supply of water from Cairnsmill Reservoir, a mile or two to the south, since 1915.

Until then, the Links depended on wells scattered over different parts of the golfing area. In 1870, it was reported that a well had been sunk at the sixth hole of the Old Course and that it provided a plentiful supply of good-quality water. In 1911, a year of severe drought, several wells were sunk on the Jubilee Course, and it was evident that there was fresh water below the courses. The supply, however, was very labour intensive: it took two men to operate one pump, and that was expensive.

The town of St Andrews did not have a gravitational water supply until 1885, when a piped supply was laid from Cairnsmill and other sources. As the town grew, that supply became inadequate, and in 1912 the Town Council acquired 103½ acres of land on high ground at Cameron, a mile or two south of Cairnsmill, with a good catchment area. In 1915 the Cameron supply came on tap and Cairnsmill was redundant.

As far back as 1903, the secretary of the R&A had asked whether the Town Council was willing to provide a supply of water for the course. At that time the Town Council was unable to meet the request, but they indicated that they might be able to do so 'in the near future'. This turned out to be about ten years later.

Some time before Cameron Reservoir became operational, the Town Council had been having discussions with the R&A about getting a supply from Cairnsmill. The R&A was keen on the idea, but the council was having problems with its community supply, and, while they were sympathetic to the R&A's wishes, they would give no assurance that water would always be available for the Links.

The two parties agreed in 1913 that pipes should be laid to all four courses, including the Eden, which was then still on the drawing board. The R&A was to bear a proportion of the cost of the pipe-laying, and, while the threat was still real that the supply would be cut off if there was a domestic shortage, the Town Council was sure that when Cameron Reservoir was commissioned, there would be enough for all purposes.

In May 1914, the council produced a scheme for watering the greens of all four courses with unfiltered water from Cairnsmill Reservoir which was to be set aside for the exclusive needs of the courses. This meant that the

Links had an independent supply that could be used in the severest drought without denying water to domestic and other users. The cost of the scheme was £3,794 and the pipe-laying began in January 1915. On 15 May of the same year, all connections with the Links water were completed and 'the greens were now independent of rain'.

The arrangement worked well for many years, but by 1966, with labour costs increasing, the Joint Links Committee, which came into being in 1953, found that even frugal watering was costly. Watering had to be done effectively at night, and hoses and sprinklers had to be moved manually, involving the payment of overtime to the staff.

The Joint Links Committee looked at the possibility of installing automatic overhead irrigation, and the burgh engineer reported that Cairnsmill had sufficient capacity to sustain such a system. It was agreed that it should be installed, in the first instance, on the Old Course at a cost of £6,000. The automatic pop-up sprinklers would be activated from a pre-set control board in the office of the Links supervisor. The system was switched on in June 1967, and by that time the cost had risen by £1,000 to £7,000.

The scheme worked well in spite of one or two hiccups, and in 1971 it was extended to the tees and greens of the Eden Course and to certain vulnerable points of fairway on the Old Course. Later still, it was extended to serve the New and Jubilee courses, and in 1978 to give a fuller fairway service to the Old Course.

Overhead sprinkler irrigation on the Old Course

By this time, the ageing Cairnsmill Reservoir, nearly a hundred years old, was beginning to feel the strain of these additional duties and was creaking, literally, at the joints. The gravitational system on its own was not able to cope with the pressure demanded, and a booster pump was installed to give it a helping hand, but it appears that over the years, when repairs were carried out, pipes of varying gauge or calibre had been used, and, while this had not made much difference in a natural flow, the weaknesses which had been created in the main were unable to meet the pressure of the booster. In the mid-1980s the Links Trust carried out a detailed examination of the reservoir and its distribution system, and they came to the conclusion that a storage tank should be provided on or near the Links with a capacity of between 150,000 and 200,000 gallons as an insurance against the failure of the supply main. This was accomplished in 1987, and at about the same time St Andrews University gave permission to the Trust to sink a borehole on their land at the North Haugh. This yielded a supply which was reported to be adequate and wholesome. One disadvantage was that the borehole was about a mile from the storage tank, which had been tucked unobtrusively into the sand dunes on the seaward side of the Jubilee's first green. It was also on the wrong side of the St Andrews–Guardbridge Road, which carries the bulk of traffic moving into St Andrews from the north and west and a high proportion of St Andrews-bound traffic from England via the Forth Road Bridge.

There were two options facing the Trust: either lay a main under the road and the golf courses to the storage tank; or pipe water from the borehole into the Swilcan Burn only a hundred or so yards away and allow it to flow to the outfall at the West Sands. A dam gate would be provided there to create a pool of water which could be pumped into the storage tank. The latter option would be the cheaper, but there would always be the possibility of contamination by pesticides, fertilisers and weedkillers, which could upset any balanced programme set by the Links supervisor, for the Swilcan Burn trickles through a mile or two of agricultural land before it sets its playful trap for the Old Course golfers.

The Trustees took a chance on it, but in August 1990 the Links Management Committee reported to the Trustees that agricultural diesel oil had been found in the Swilcan and they asked for additional finance to allow water to be conveyed directly from the borehole to the pumping station which had been installed at the mouth of the Swilcan.

The search for new sources of water continued and a new borehole was sunk on the edge of the Balgove Course, which avoided the problem of going under the St Andrews to Guardbridge road. The flow was both strong and wholesome, and the water was piped directly to the storage tank, avoiding the danger of agricultural contamination. Storage capacity was increased to

357,000 gallons, and in times of summer drought up to one million gallons a night could be sprayed onto the courses.

By 1997, however, the drive to improve course quality had made the existing sprinkler system – which had developed piecemeal over the years – obsolete. In particular, it was difficult to control, being either 'on' or 'off' for each course. The improvement in the Trust's financial position by this time made possible a comprehensive programme to provide a new 'hi-tech' solution.

The need for reliable irrigation in the face of the capricious British weather has been the Trust's concern ever since its formation in 1974. By 1995, boreholes had been sunk and a reservoir built with a storage capacity of 357,000 gallons, but more was needed. The first phase of the resulting search was completed early in 1999 and the second in 2001.

A new reservoir was built beside the existing storage tank to the west of the Jubilee Greenkeeping Centre, increasing capacity to 750,000 gallons. A main water pipeline was laid in a trench dug across the courses linking the reservoir with boreholes sunk on the west side of the Links. Individually controlled sprinkler heads were installed, first on the Eden, Strathtyrum and Balgove courses in 1999, and, in 2001, on the Old, New and Jubilee courses.

Laying the main pipeline across all the courses

It was a state-of-the-art irrigation system incorporating a weather station, recording data such as humidity, ground temperature, rainfall and wind speed, so if there was a sudden change in weather, the sprinklers could be regulated as required. It was a testing experience for the greenkeepers because with more than 4,000 sprinkler heads to control and 700 acres of Links to nurture, they had to be trained to use the sophisticated computer-control system which was recognised as one of the very finest. It was so refined it could be operated from the office or by hand-held radio. The day of the labourer/gardener/greenkeeper who could push a lawnmower was well and truly gone.

A valuable by-product of the installation was that it enabled the Millennium Open construction team to locate and map underground services such as electricity cables and pipelines.

THE LADIES' GOLF CLUB

St Andrews has been claimed to be the birthplace of ladies' golf. Whether or not this claim can be sustained, it is certainly true that a Ladies' Golf Club was formed in St Andrews in 1867, even though golf, as we acknowledge it today, was not played by the original members over their home course. The game they played was putting – over the land on the seaward side of the second tee of the Old Course known as the Himalayas because of its hummocky layout.

The club came into being with the friendly co-operation of the Royal and Ancient Golf Club, with whom the Ladies' Club have always maintained a friendly if monastic affinity.

Long before 1860, the golf caddies formed a crude, short putting circuit quite close to the Old Course on the site of what later became Rusacks Marine Hotel. There they played for halfpennies when times were good, or just for fun when money was tight. But when the caddies were busy, the putting course was unused and a few of the more venturesome ladies went on to the caddies' course. Two of the ringleaders were the wife and sister of a well-known R&A member, Lieutenant-Colonel Boothby.

Ladies putting on what appears to be a cold, blustery day (George Washington Wilson Collection)

ABOVE AND BELOW: Matches on the Ladies' Course (the Himalayas) attracted keen interest

It often happened that while the ladies were amusing themselves on the caddies' course, the 'rightful tenants' appeared, but the ladies were not easily to be dislodged; they had been joined, or perhaps reinforced, by others, all thoroughly enjoying themselves while the caddies looked on in sullen but silent disapproval. It was not in the caddies' best interests to protest, for there was a long-standing, if tenuous, bond between a caddie and 'his man', and it was not unusual for a player's wife to help his caddie in times of hardship.

So it was an uneasy peace which reigned, with the caddies being elbowed out of their own putting green. But even mute protests may be sympathetically received, and about 1866 Mr D.L. Burn, another prominent R&A member, suggested that perhaps some corner of the Links might be found where the ladies could play their game away from the critical and accusing eye. It was Mrs Boothby herself who suggested that such a quiet spot existed just across the Swilcan Burn. The R&A agreed, and the Ladies' Course (or putting green) was laid out. It should be borne in mind that the Links at that time had not been repossessed by the Town Council but was in the ownership of Mr Cheape of Strathtyrum, who allowed the R&A to maintain it. In the same year, 1867, a Ladies' Golf Club was formed to run the course with an original membership restricted to 100 ladies and 50 gentlemen. The R&A imposed a nominal rental for the use of the land.

For nearly a century the green was used exclusively by the members. There was a fear in 1894, when St Andrews Town Council regained the Links, that the ladies would be dispossessed but the council gave the club its blessing – and claimed the nominal rental which had been imposed by the club.

Some time after the Second World War, the ladies began, apparently, to feel the effects of post-war financial strain, and they opened up their green to the public, who were allowed to play on payment of a green fee. The Himalayas Putting Green proved to be highly popular, especially with visitors, for it provided more interest and more shelter than the flat, exposed municipal putting green on the neighbouring Bruce Embankment. The enjoyment which the Himalayas provide is not confined to holidaymakers alone, and in 1994 former US president George H.W. Bush derived so much pleasure from his first round that he immediately requested a second.

The good relationship established between the Town Council and the club also continued with the Links Trust, which in 1994 agreed to an extended lease of 22 years to what was now called the Ladies' Putting Club.

OVERLEAF: The rain has passed and the Himalayas
Putting Green is quickly crowded (Masakuni Akiyama)

THE SECOND WORLD WAR

The fate of the golf courses was nearly sealed during the Second World War. Home-grown food was urgently required, and any land that was able to support a blade of grass was expected to be used to its full capacity.

By 1942 the Department of Agriculture had got round to looking at the potential of golf courses as grazing land. Not unnaturally, they expected every part of the courses to be used, and that, apart from greens and teeing grounds, grass should not be cut but should be left for grazing. This came as a great shock to St Andrews Town Council. To leave the Old Course to go to seed was on the same level of vandalism as bombing Rome or Florence, and they prepared a strong case for submission to the department. They claimed that it would be better for grazing if the fairways were cut, and that if there was no grass-cutting the most famous golf course in the world, as well as the other St Andrews courses, would become hayfields. The council had spent thousands of pounds on the development of the Jubilee Course, and because that development had been arrested, weeds were growing. Unless they were cut, they would choke the grass. St Andrews was a wartime centre for the training of young servicemen and women, and the golf courses were an important recreational outlet for these young people. These would become unplayable if no cutting was carried out.

The Town Council also pointed out that they already had a grazing tenant on the Links. They were willing to co-operate in food production, and they had already made arrangements with their grazing tenant to increase the number of sheep on the Links from 150 to 200. Finally, the council contended that if the courses remained uncut, there would be a serious loss of revenue to the Town Council without any compensating advantage in food production. The department accepted the council's views and the courses were saved.

IV

THE PEOPLE WHO MADE THE LINKS

THE CADDIES

In nineteenth-century St Andrews, the caddies' lot was generally not a happy one. Although they might have been happy in their work, they were effectively social outcasts. Having no regular job and no security of employment, they lived in a state of poverty which bordered on destitution.

Before the 1894 Links Act came into force, the R&A took a paternal interest in the caddies: members of the club made gifts of food and fuel during severe weather and passed on articles of clothing which had served their days in the corridors of commerce or golf. Life, thanks to a little patronising charity, was bearable, but only just. The club did its best to organise the caddies by drawing up a set of rules for their engagement, appointing a caddie master whose job it was to regulate the distribution of work, maintain a rota of employment and to uphold discipline. Justice was often summary: a complaint meant automatic guilt, and there was no appeal. The R&A, however, established a Benefit Fund, to which they subscribed generously, and to which the caddies themselves were expected to contribute – at the rate of fourpence a week in the busy summer season and twopence a week in the off season.

They also fixed rates of pay. In 1771, the fees of fore-caddies and carrying caddies were fixed at fourpence for going the length of the Hole o' Cross (the fifth) and sixpence – 'and no more' – if they had to go farther. The penalty for any member of the club transgressing the rule, upwards or downwards, was quite severe – 'they are to pay two pint bottles of claret at the first meeting they attend'.

In 1875, the club brought out *Rules Regarding the Pay and Discipline of Caddies*, under which 'first-class' caddies were to be paid 1s 6d for a round and 1s (five pence in today's currency) for each following round, or part thereof. 'Second-class' caddies were to receive 1s for the first round and sixpence for the second round. During the spring and autumn meetings of the club the fee was 2s for each round.

St Andrews Town Council took an interest – sometimes a distant interest – in the welfare of the caddies, and in 1868 Lieutenant-Colonel George Moncrieff, who was provost of the town, worked out a scheme of his own for providing some sort of basic education for them. This took the form of evening classes in the Fishers School located near the cathedral ruins. They

LEFT: Reid Jack after holing a 10-yard putt on the 18th green in the inaugural World Amateur Team Championship for the Eisenhower Trophy in October 1958. Great Britain and Ireland (J.B. Carr, R.R. Jack, A.H. Perowne and G.B. Wolstenholme) finished third, on 919, behind Australia and the USA, who tied at 918. Australia won the play-off (D.C. Thomson)

A group of caddies during the 1920s

were open to all registered caddies. Twenty-seven caddies enrolled for the opening session, and at the end of the session a prize list was published. The best reader and best writer got 12s each, the best attenders got 10s, and the best behaved got 8s each. The catch was that no cash was placed in the palm of the winner, but was credited to their 'clothing fund', which was held by Mr Forgan of clubmaking fame.

With the passing of the 1894 Links Act, the patronage of the R&A diminished and responsibility devolved to the Town Council or, rather, the magistrates, which meant that the caddies came under the jurisdiction of the Burgh Court through special bye-laws. The first set of rules for the licensing of caddies came before the Town Council in 1896, and these were almost an exact copy of those in force at Musselburgh. The Town Council was in agreement with the rules, but they appeared to be more concerned about young people entering the caddie ranks. They felt it was a 'dead-end job', and they were of the opinion that no boy under 15 years of age should be allowed to caddie except during school holidays, and boys of 15 to 17 should only be allowed to caddie in special circumstances.

Their principal concern was that caddying, in the eyes of youngsters, was a more attractive and carefree way of life than learning a trade. There was also trouble from enterprising youngsters who waylaid golfers at the railway station, thus avoiding the 'normal channels of employment' through the caddie master.

The regulations then adopted stipulated that no person should act as a caddie for hire until licensed by the magistrates; licensed caddies had to wear an officially numbered badge; they must not refuse an engagement, canvass for employment, quarrel or make a noise about their rotation, or about the players or the game or annoy the public or players in any way; and they had to be decently clothed and strictly sober, and conduct themselves in a civil, respectful and proper manner. Caddies convicted of crime would forfeit their licence. The regulations also determined the tariff payable to the caddies and prescribed that 'licences are granted on condition that the regulations shall be observed and caddies contravening them are liable on conviction before the magistrates in a penalty not exceeding 10s for each offence or seven days' imprisonment, or to suspension or revocation of their licence'.

Arnold Palmer and his caddie, Tip Anderson, crossing the wooden bridge over the Swilcan Burn (St Andrews University)

While the Town Council laid down strict regulations with severe penalties for defaulters, the caddies' lot had not greatly improved. The caddies were not 'employed' by the Town Council, and their livelihood was just as precarious as it had always been. Socially, they were shunned: local golf clubs would not admit them as members or even as guests of members.

The caddie's badge was a cumbersome brass plate mounted on a heavy leather armband which he was supposed to wear at all times when he was engaged or waiting for an engagement. It was like a leper's sign which set him apart from other human beings. If he did not wear it, he was liable to be summoned before the magistrates.

In 1903, a clubmaker who took a player onto the Links to give him a golf lesson carried his patron's clubs between shots, and for that he was taken to court and charged with carrying clubs for hire while not having been licensed to do so. Even the great and formidable Andra' Kirkaldy did not escape the attention of the courts. In 1904 Andra' had been playing as a hired professional with the Earl of Dudley, then Lord Lieutenant of Ireland, but one day His Excellency wanted to try out his newly learned techniques against his clubhouse peers and invited Andra' to be his caddie. Andra' went to the caddie master, Alex Taylor, and told him of the invitation. Mr Taylor replied that rules were rules and that he could

Lord Brabazon of Tara prepares to take the first caddie cart down the first fairway of the Old Course in 1949

not act as a caddie without a badge. Andra', however, had scant respect for trivial authority, and out he went the following day without licence or badge to caddie for Lord Dudley. He was duly summoned to appear in court, where he made a plea of not guilty to the charge of carrying clubs for hire without a licence.

Since police evidence was unable to show that Andra' had been paid for his services, the court found Andra' not guilty. The magistrates must have had their own suspicions, for they took the opportunity of issuing a public warning that no one was allowed to carry clubs without having a badge to show that he was licensed.

The fact that the magistrates were prepared to deal with breaches of the caddies' regulations showed that they were disposed to protect the caddies' interests even though they showed scant respect for them in other ways.

They were prepared to carry the banner for them in 1903 when a petition was submitted to the Town Council by a group of R&A members. The club members complained about 'the general behaviour of the caddies, who recently seem to have got entirely out of hand'. They claimed there had been numerous cases of caddies in weekly employment failing to turn up on time, declining to caddie at the regulation tariff, refusing to clean the clubs and using grossly impertinent language. They complained also that club members had greater difficulty in obtaining the services of a caddie than non-members.

Provost George Murray sympathised with the caddies 'to some extent' for he was well aware that they avoided the club members in the expectation of getting more than the ordinary tariff from strangers. And he went on to say that the club members were at fault because they broke the rules by not engaging and paying the caddie through the caddie master; some of them engaged their caddie a considerable time before they intended to play, and this represented a hardship to the caddie, who was not paid for waiting time. This had led to bad feeling between caddies and club members. He suggested that the members should hire their caddies through the caddie master a few minutes before they were due to play.

Although the Town Council had no deep affection for the caddies, they were clearly not prepared to place them on any sacrificial altar. A few weeks after the previous complaints, four members of the R&A wrote to the Town

Council listing complaints against a number of the caddies, who were duly summoned before the council to give their side of the story. After hearing the caddies, the council told the complaining members that if they had observed the bye-laws, no cause for complaint need ever have arisen. This would appear to suggest that the Town Council had adopted a paternal attitude towards the caddies. This was reflected in a licensing meeting of the magistrates in 1903, when the caddies were given a fatherly briefing by Bailie John Milne, who told them that the magistrates insisted upon every caddie washing his face and hands and brushing his boots and clothes before going to the Links each morning. 'A man's clothing may be shabby,' he told them, 'but that is no reason why they should not be clean.' A few months later, in September 1903, the Sheriff of Fife approved a bye-law which confirmed the R&A's 1875 'Rules' establishing two classes of caddies and setting the fees per round.

In the following year, the caddies petitioned the Town Council to have a shelter erected at the Links, suggesting a location near the flagstaff. This was the area lying behind and to the east of the 18th green. The flagstaff belonged to the R&A and from it was flown the club's standard. It was a focal point for the caddies and other members of the community enjoying the passing scene.

Golfers and their caddies on the 18th tee of the Old Course

Provost Murray was not keen to have a shelter on that site, for the ground was part of the town's common and should not be allocated for the exclusive use of one section of the community. The Town Council, however, decided that the shelter should be built in the north-east corner of the ground and that it should be contiguous with the caddie master's office. To allay misgivings about allocating public ground for the exclusive use of the caddies, the council designated the building as a public shelter 'because the public would have the right to shelter under the veranda'.

A new and relaxed relationship between the caddies and the Town Council seemed to be developing, for some of the misdemeanours, such as neglecting to wear the caddies' badge, appeared to have been ignored or overlooked, and, while the caddies seemed to be quite happy about this, other people who had not been licensed to caddie began to appear on the scene, poaching work which the caddies regarded as theirs. This practice gathered momentum until, early in 1912, the regular caddies voiced their disapproval, and their complaint was taken to the Town Council. The regular caddies felt it was unfair that they should take up their places at the Links for the whole year, and yet when the busy time came around they were put on the same level as casual, unlicensed caddies. One of the councillors made the suggestion that the regular caddies should be given a badge 'to distinguish them from the casuals'.

The provost made it clear that there was no deprivation of work affecting the regular caddies, for they were sent out first, and only when the regular rota was exhausted were the casuals considered. Badges were provided for the caddies but they were less obtrusive than the old leather-and-brass creations. They were made of aluminium, round, about the size of a ten-pence piece and could be pinned out of sight on the reverse of the jacket lapel.

The role of the caddie in St Andrews began to fade after 1949, when Lord Brabazon of Tara introduced the caddie cart to the Links, and shortly afterwards the Town Council dispensed with the services of the caddie master, devolving his duties on the Old Course starter. But if the caddies diminished in quantity, their quality and status improved.

Commercialisation of golf led to better conditions for professional golfers, and this in turn affected the caddies. The best professionals wanted more than bag carriers: they wanted technicians who knew the game and the tools of the trade; people who knew the courses and their subtleties; people who were physically fit for an exacting job and mentally equipped to deal with the stresses of the professional game. Two such outstanding men in the St Andrews post-war era were Wallace (Guy) Gillespie, who had a long and warm partnership with the Australian Peter Thomson, and James (Tip)

RIGHT: Peter Thomson with Guy Gillespie

Anderson, who was Arnold Palmer's right-hand man on his visits to this country. There were, of course, other caddies like Guy and Tip in different parts of the country who became almost as well known as the professionals for whom they caddied.

When caddie carts were blamed for damaging the golfing turf, they were banned from the Old Course, and the demand for caddies reappeared in the 1980s. The number of caddies increased until the Links Trust decided that a caddie master should again be employed. By 2008, the demand for caddies, particularly on the Old Course, had become so strong that the number licensed by the Trust was coming close to 200 a year. The primitive facilities behind the 18th green of the Old Course had been replaced with an improved shelter located on the Bruce Embankment offering modern changing accommodation.

The caddies were now drawn from many strata of Scottish society and, increasingly, from abroad. In addition to the regulars, St Andrews students found it a good way to earn some money in the long summer vacation, sometimes putting in three rounds a day, and women as well as men were drawn to the carrying trade. This large influx of would-be caddies caused a problem, however. The visiting golfer had been led by all he had read about St Andrews to expect to be helped around the course by an expert on the courses and how to play them, as well as a polished raconteur on Links lore.

Women caddies became a regular feature of golf at St Andrews in the twentieth century

The solution was the introduction in 2001 of a week-long training course in the classroom covering the etiquette of the game, the history and role of the caddie, the Rules of Golf, how to compile yardage data, and how to look after the golfer. Theory was followed by practice, which involved caddying at a reduced fee for 30 rounds, with the golfer completing an assessment form at the end on all aspects of the trainee's performance. Successful trainees became fully fledged caddies, with even a qualification recognised by the Scottish Qualifications Authority.

Details of the caddie training course were advertised on the Trust's website, and the response was immediate, with enquiries coming from home and abroad. By the end of the 2008 season, over 300 trainees had succeeded in achieving the 'St Andrews Standard' qualification, entitling them to receive the full caddie fee and, if the golfer was satisfied, a healthy gratuity on top.

Caddies had been emerging from the social darkness since the early 1930s. At that time the caddies included dropouts, unemployables, fishermen forced by the collapse of their own industry to seek an existence on land, and, of course, the unfortunate victims of the industrial depression of that period. But caddies were caddies – assessed by their lowest denominator. Happily, all that has changed and within a decade or two the caddies had hoisted themselves to a dignity which was denied to their predecessors. The image of the scruffy, intellectually deprived caddie is destroyed.

THE PEOPLE WHO BROUGHT
THE LINKS TO LIFE

THE MORRIS FAMILY

Any reference to the men who built the reputation of St Andrews as the Mecca of Golf must begin with the Morrises.

Old Tom, of course, was the patriarch. He was four times winner of the Open Championship, and this is how the world of golf tends to remember him. But his contribution to the game and to St Andrews goes far beyond his skill as a golfer.

Tom Morris was born in St Andrews on 16 June 1821, the son of John Morris and Jean Bruce. Like many professionals of his day, he was a skilled club- and ballmaker, and to these skills he added the arts of greenkeeping and golf course layout. As custodian of the Links, he fashioned the Old and New courses as the world knows them today.

When he returned to St Andrews from Prestwick in 1864, he found a different Old Course. Two holes had been cut on most of the greens in order to speed up play, so Tom took it as his duty to adapt the course to the new scheme of things. He widened the greens to give outgoing and incoming players more comfortable conditions and then – with his barrow, his spade and his shovel – he set about widening the fairways, which were covered by whin bushes. It was hard, back-breaking work, which Tom undertook quietly, quickly and without fuss. He was quick to learn that the secret of maintaining links turf in its natural condition is to keep the soil poor, using sand as a medium. His words to his foreman, David Honeyman, became well known in St Andrews: 'Saund, Honeyman, saund, and then mair saund.' Sand by the barrowload was heaped on the greens in wintertime, to produce the fine putting grasses which are a feature of all good seaside links.

He devised his own method of returfing greens such as the sixth and seventh, which consisted mainly of heathery fibre. When he returfed the sixth green, he laid the turf he had removed on the Elysian Fields (the plateau which forms part of the 14th fairway), and within two years it had recovered all the fine qualities required for putting. This turf he used for resurfacing the seventh green.

Tom claimed that the idea of having iron linings for the holes was his. The idea was born, he said, when he returfed the High Hole (the seventh). He said that because of the soft nature of the ground there, the hole quickly became enlarged, and it could never be kept in order for any length of time. He said, 'I got the blacksmith to make an iron rim, which I put into the hole, and that kept it in perfect order. Now they are used all over the world.' When he was not returfing greens, he was planning and creating bunkers to add interest and intriguing difficulty to the new holes.

A St Andrews native, Tom learned club- and ballmaking under the great Allan Robertson. Some historians have made much of the supposed rift between these two great men over the advent of the gutta ball in 1848. There is no doubt they had a disagreement, Tom seeing the gutta – cheap and indestructible – as the ball of the future, and Allan regarding it as a threat to his long-established featherie-ball business. But it is hard to believe that they quarrelled so bitterly that they never again spoke to one another, for both were mild-mannered men not given to excesses of speech or action. Tom left Allan's business and set up on his own, making guttas and featheries. Shortly afterwards, Allan started to make guttas, and so the rift was quickly healed. Indeed, Tom and Allan played many matches together after their contretemps in 1848.

Tom married Agnes Bayne (Nancy to her friends), the daughter of a coachman at Kincaple, a mansion house a mile or two from the Links. The ceremony was performed by the Revd Principal Haldane of St Mary's College,

ABOVE LEFT: The grand old man of golf, Tom Morris (D.C. Thomson)

ABOVE RIGHT: In 1901, aged 80, posing for a studio photograph

Old Tom Morris chats to Provost George Murray on the 18th fairway of the Old Course outside the New Golf Club. Provost Murray captained the New Golf Club in 1904 and 1905. Tom died in 1908 as a result of an accident in the clubhouse. A fortnight later Provost Murray was killed falling from his bicycle

who was also minister of the First Charge of Holy Trinity Church, St Andrews – the same man who had baptised him in 1821 and who is credited by some with having provided the name for the notorious Principal's Nose bunker at the 16th. The wedding took place at 2 Playfair Terrace, where Nancy was in domestic service. The marriage was a happy one but along its course were landmarks of sorrow. The first-born child, Thomas, died in April 1850 at the age of four – infant mortality was very high in the nineteenth century. Shortly after Thomas's death, another son was born – also named Thomas – on 20 April 1851. This was the Tommy who was to win the Open Championship four times. He was baptised three weeks later by Dr John Craig, who was an assistant at Holy Trinity Church, St Andrews. An extract from the Register of Births and Baptisms shows that Tommy was named 'Thomas Moris, son of Thomas Moris, golf ball maker, and Agnes Byne his wife'. Witnesses at the baptism were Jane Bruce and Mrs Kirk. It will be noted that the surname of father and son is written with one 'r' and that the 'a' has been omitted from the name of the mother, Agnes Bayne.

Tommy grew to be a strong, handsome youth, and his four Open Championship successes included the triple win which gave him ownership of the Championship Belt. Tommy learned his early golf at Prestwick, for in 1851, shortly after Tommy's birth, Old Tom was invited by Colonel James Ogilvie Fairlie to become keeper of the green at Prestwick.

Tom stayed at Prestwick for 14 years, before returning to St Andrews in 1865 to become custodian of the Links for the R&A at a salary of £50 a year. Tom was keen to find a deeper security for his wife and family, and in March 1866, when G.D. Brown announced his intention to retire from his club- and ballmaking business, Tom bought him out and founded his own successful business.

Tom retired as custodian of the Links in 1903, but a year earlier Sir George Reid was commissioned by the R&A to paint Tom's portrait for a fee of £250. The club had always treated Tom with the greatest respect and generosity, and in 1896 they opened an Annuity Fund, which raised a total of £1,240. This was used to purchase an annuity for Tom of £100, which he was to receive in addition to his salary.

Tom's death in 1908 was one of golf's great tragedies. He was an honorary member of the New Golf Club, which had been formed six years earlier, in 1902, and it was his custom to walk to the clubhouse each morning for a chat with his cronies and to cast an eye over the newspapers. On Sunday, 24 May, Tom was chatting as usual in the clubhouse. He rose and walked to the passage, and almost immediately his friends heard him fall and call out. They found him unconscious at the foot of the cellar steps which led from the passage. He had sustained severe injuries to the base of his skull and died a few minutes after admission to the Memorial Cottage Hospital, St Andrews. It appears that Tom had mistaken the cellar door for the toilet door, missed his footing and fallen. Tom was 87 years of age, and his eyesight had dimmed a little; but it was an accident which might easily have happened to a younger man.

Tom's funeral service was held in St Mary's Church because the parish church, Holy Trinity, of which Tom was an elder, was undergoing major restoration. Golf clubs all over the country subscribed towards a memorial, which took the form of the endowment of a bed in the Freddie Tait Ward of the St Andrews Memorial Hospital where Tom died. Freddie Tait was another golfing legend, who had been killed in action eight years earlier, in 1900, fighting the Boers at Koodoosberg Drift. He was twice Amateur champion, he enjoyed meeting and beating the best professionals, and he was the first man to score level fours – 72 – on the Old Course. He was serving as a lieutenant in The Black Watch when he was killed. The news of his death shocked St Andrews, and his memory was perpetuated in the Freddie Tait Ward.

Tom was succeeded as custodian of the Links by Hugh Hamilton, greenkeeper at Portrush, who had been head gardener to Andrew Carnegie, the great industrialist and philanthropist, before spending a short time as greenkeeper at North Berwick.

The glory and the tragedy of Tommy Morris's short life have been often related. His wife, Margaret Drennan, to whom he was devoted, died in childbirth on 11 September 1875 while Tommy and his father were playing at North

Old Tom Morris's funeral cortège winds its way to Tom's family grave. The coffin and its bearers are passing the obelisk erected in memory of Allan Robertson

Tommy Morris
wearing the
Championship Belt

Berwick against the Park brothers. Tommy, heartbroken, played little golf after the death of his wife, and a few weeks later, on Christmas Day 1875, he was found dead in bed at his father's house at 6 Pilmuir Links. He had spent Christmas Eve with a few friends, returning home about 11 p.m., apparently in good health. He spent a short time talking with his mother who, by this time, had become a chair-bound invalid, and then retired to bed. Next morning, he was found dead, a trickle of blood coming from his mouth. A post-mortem examination revealed that he had died because of the bursting of a blood vessel in his right lung.

The news of Tommy's death came as a shock to golfers everywhere, and a committee was formed locally to provide a suitable memorial. Contributions were made by golf clubs and societies, and eventually the committee accepted the design of Mr John Rhind, an Edinburgh sculptor, for a monumental tombstone to be erected in the Cathedral Burying Ground. The design was worked out in Binny stone, showing Tommy in bas-relief about three-quarters' life size in a characteristic pose, wearing a golfing jacket and a 'Scotch cap', the accepted golfing headgear of the era, preparing to play a shot to the hole. Beneath the relief was carved an inscription written at the request of the committee by the Very Revd Principal Tulloch:

> In memory of Tommy, son of Thomas Morris, who died 25 December 1875 aged 24 years – deeply regretted by numerous friends and all golfers. He, three times in succession, won the Championship Belt and held it without rivalry and yet without envy, his many amiable qualities being no less acknowledged than his golfing achievements. This monument has been erected by contributions from 60 golfing societies.

The memorial was unveiled at a ceremony after the R&A autumn meeting on Tuesday, 24 September 1878. The address was given by the Lord Justice General John Inglis, captain of the club, before a congregation of several hundreds, including representatives of many golf clubs. The unveiling ceremony was carried out by a Miss Phelps acting on behalf of Tommy's only sister, Mrs Elizabeth Hunter.

During his lifetime, Tommy worked in his father's shop, making golf clubs and balls, and he is credited with the invention of the niblick. Although he was the world's greatest exponent of the lofted shot to the green, it is unlikely that he invented the iron niblick, or 8 iron, as it is known today, for Tommy made wooden clubs, not cleeks. Clubmaking and cleekmaking are two completely different crafts. It is likely, however, that Tommy was the first to make the wooden niblick or brassie niblick, as it was later known. The story is told that when R.J.B. Tait of Aberlady was playing with Tommy, his driver broke, exposing part of the lead and bone. Tommy took the club to his workshop, filed the broken head to give it loft and fitted a shorter shaft. For the protection of the club, he fitted a brass plate to the sole. When next Tommy went to Aberlady, he had two wooden niblicks, one of which he presented to Mr Tait. W.T. Linskill, who retired to St Andrews after founding the Cambridge University Golfing Society, described the wooden niblick thus:

> The wooden niblick has a shaft similar to that of the driver. It is well spooned and very short from heel to toe, but the head is broad. A ball may be lying in a small hollow, or in a rut, into which none of the other clubs, by reason of their length of head, could possibly descend so as to dislodge the ball. The wooden niblick is the club for this purpose.

Old Tom's sorrows continued with the death of his beloved Nancy at the age of 61. It happened on 1 November 1876, only 11 months after Tommy's death, and there can be little doubt that the death of her son accelerated her own.

The memorial erected to Young Tom Morris over his grave in the cathedral grounds

One of the brighter spots in Tom's life was the marriage in February 1875 of his only daughter, Elizabeth, to James Hunter of Darien, Georgia, USA. A 26-year-old timber merchant, James Hunter was a native of Prestwick, son of William Hunter, a hotel-keeper. He was a talented amateur golfer and a shrewd businessman who developed strong commercial links at home and overseas, particularly in the United States. The couple set up home in Darien, but their first child, Tommy Morris Hunter, was only two months old when he died. A short time after the death of Elizabeth's mother, Elizabeth and James returned to St Andrews and set up home with Tom in Pilmuir Links. James made frequent business trips abroad, and he was in

Mobile, Alabama, when he died on 31 January 1886 at the age of 37, leaving Elizabeth with three young children. Elizabeth was only 46 when she died at her father's house in June 1898.

Elizabeth's daughter, Agnes Bayne Hunter, inherited longevity from her grandfather. She married W.J. Rusack, a prominent St Andrews man who served for some years as a member of St Andrews Town Council. She was 83 when she died on 29 June 1960 in a hospital near Cupar.

Jack Morris, the youngest son of Tom and Agnes, died suddenly on 22 February 1883. Jack had a deformity of the legs which prevented his participation in the game, but he took an active interest in everything pertaining to it and was an acknowledged authority on golf, in addition to being a skilled club- and ballmaker. He died quite suddenly of a heart attack.

Jamie Morris, their third son, was christened James Ogilvie Fairlie Morris, as a gesture of respect to Colonel James Ogilvie Fairlie, under whose patronage Tom had gone to Prestwick in 1851. As a young man, Jamie was probably the most stylish golfer of all the Morrises. But he never achieved the honours which fell to his father and his brother, though he came close to winning the Open Championship at Prestwick in 1876. In the second and final round he stood on the 17th tee requiring two sixes for an unassailable score, but he finished with a 9 and a 6. His score held the lead for some time, but it was overtaken, first by Bob Kirk and later by Jamie Anderson.

Unlike his father, Jamie was an excellent putter, and in 1887 he equalled Tommy's record score of 77. His golfing career was cut short by rheumatism, and latterly the only connection he had with the game was in the management of the family business. Because of his poor health, his death in 1906 was not entirely unexpected. Jamie was 53 and unmarried. There was an unfortunate incident in his blameless life in 1880 following the notorious Links Road case. It was a time when feelings and passions about rights on the Links were at boiling point. Posts had been erected at Links Road to form a boundary between the golf course and the road. Jamie was one of those who felt that the posts infringed local rights, and he and three others pulled out some of the posts. All four appeared in court, and, while verdicts of not proven were given in the case of three of the accused (who were released), Jamie was found guilty and sentenced to ten days' imprisonment. In making their judgement, the magistrates stated that they would normally have imposed a fine, but if they did so in this case, the fine would be paid by 'someone else'. Jamie appealed successfully to the Court of Justiciary against the conviction, and his name was cleared.

Towards the end of 1926 and the beginning of 1927, a group of wealthy Americans tried to buy Tom Morris's shop in Links Road overlooking the

18th green. One story current at the time was that they proposed to take it down, stone by stone, and rebuild it in America as a golf club. At that time, the property belonged to W. Bruce Hunter, son of Elizabeth and grandson of Old Tom. The offer made to Mr Hunter was not disclosed, but according to him it 'was a very tempting one'. When he learned that it was to be used as a club for Americans, he refused to sell. It is interesting to note that Bruce Hunter inherited his name from his great-grandmother – Old Tom's mother – who was Jean Bruce of Anstruther.

THE CHEAPE FAMILY

The influence of the Cheape family of Strathtyrum on the golf links of St Andrews receives scant acknowledgement from those who use the Links most frequently; and none at all from those who view the Links from afar. Yet their contribution has been immeasurable; few of the developments on the St Andrews golf courses could have been accomplished without their co-operation.

The family influence began in 1782, when James Cheape of Wellfield acquired Strathtyrum Estate, which adjoins the southern boundary of the Links. James Cheape was a competent golfer, and in 1787 he won the Silver Club, which carried with it the captaincy of the Society of St Andrews Golfers. He performed a service to the golfing community in 1821 when he purchased the golf links from Charles and Cathcart Dempster, ending the notorious Rabbit Wars and saving the Links from becoming a massive rabbit warren.

James Cheape died just three years later – in 1824 – and he was succeeded by his brother, George Cheape, 20 years his junior, who had captained the society in 1801 and was the first to warn the Town Council of the damage which the rabbits were causing to the Links. George was Laird of Strathtyrum until his death in 1850 when the estate passed to his third son, George Clark Cheape of Wellfield. He died without issue and was succeeded by his brother, Alexander Cheape of Lathockar. Alexander was 44 years old when he married the daughter of the eighth Viscount Arbuthnott, and the marriage produced a son and three daughters. Alexander Cheape died in 1892 at the age of 89.

His only son, James Cheape, took over as Laird of Strathtyrum, and it is probably to him that St Andrews owes most. He was more interested in the management of his estates than he was in golf, although he was a member of the R&A. He was 39 when he succeeded to the estate in 1892, and in the following year he entered into negotiations for the sale of the Links – at least that part of the golfing area which lay west and north of the Swilcan Burn. The R&A and the Town Council of St Andrews were the prospective purchasers, and James opted to sell to the club for £5,000 rather than to the Town Council, who had offered £4,500. He was a shrewd businessman but his drive was tempered by a moderating sense of community awareness.

In negotiating the sale, James Cheape obtained all the usual constraints which are contained in a feu disposition – the legal contract concerned with the sale – and several others which were to become important in the following century. These included a ban on the erection of anything on the Links except wooden shelters for golfers, the right to dig shells from the shell pits at the mouth of the River Eden, the right of his family and guests at Strathtyrum to play golf on the New Course free of charge, and a right of pre-emption at £5,000 on the Links should the club ever decide to part with it.

Except for the right of pre-emption, these conditions became law when they were incorporated in the 1894 Links Act, under which the Town Council was empowered to purchase the Links from the R&A. Indeed, the right to free golf over the New Course was extended in the Act to cover the Old Course and any other courses which might be formed. In the 1913 Act, the right of the proprietor of Strathtyrum to six starting times daily on any of the courses – including the Old Course – was specified, presumably to ensure access when the courses were crowded. It was this particular right which was to cause the greatest concern in the future. The same rights were included in the feu disposition by which James Cheape sold land to the Town Council in 1936. This land had been leased by Mr Cheape to the town in

Workers from the Strathtyrum estate in March 1963 exercising the laird's right to dig shells from the shell pits on the Eden Course, near the estuary of the River Eden, which forms the western boundary of the Links. The shells were used for surfacing carriageways on the Strathtyrum estate. (The author Tom Jarrett is second from the right) (St Andrews University)

1913 to form the Eden Course. The right to free golf and six starting times a day meant little to James Cheape personally, for although he played golf only occasionally, what he did play was available to him free as a member of the R&A, and it was revealed at the 1946 tribunal that he had never exercised his statutory right.

James Cheape was 44 years old when, on 22 December 1897, he married Lady Griselda Ogilvy, daughter of the seventh Earl of Airlie. The union produced two sons and a daughter. When James Cheape died in 1943, at the age of 89, the estate passed to the elder of his two sons, Alexander Ogilvy Cheape, known to his friends, family and the whole of St Andrews as Zander. Like his father, he married late in life: he was 53 when he married Miss Gladys Prodgers of Barbados. Zander was a life member of the R&A, but although he had a locker in the clubhouse he never owned a set of golf clubs to put in it. He died without issue in April 1981 at the age of 82, and Strathtyrum Estate passed to his widow. Part of the estate had already passed to Mrs Cheape, for it was she who in 1971 sold to the Town Council the land on which the first Balgove Course was formed.

While the Cheape family remained in control of Strathtyrum Estate, St Andrews Links Trust was confident that the rights and privileges conferred by a succession of Links Acts would be exercised, as they had always been, with restraint. But fears lurked in the minds of the Trustees and the townspeople that some day the estate might fall into the hands of entrepreneurs who would not be so sensitive in their use of the privileges. Indeed, rumour was rife in the early 1990s that a Japanese consortium was interested in the estate for the sole purpose of exploiting the right to the six starting times each day on the Old Course and to free golf on all the courses. It would have been theoretically possible for almost 7,000 rounds of golf to be played over the Old Course in a typical year by any proprietor of Strathtyrum and his or her guests. The Trust entered into protracted negotiations with Mrs Gladys Cheape to buy out the rights – which was permitted by mutual agreement under the 1974 Act – and agreement was reached in 1992.

All worries about future exploitation of the Strathtyrum rights for gain were laid once and for all to rest, and it was with some relief that the townspeople learned of the agreement with Mrs Cheape. The Annual Report of the Links Trust in 1993 indicated that Mrs Cheape had relinquished her rights for a total of £245,000 payable at the rate of £35,000 per year until 1998.

There are two permanent reminders of the Cheape family's contribution to St Andrew Links. The first is Cheape's bunker on the 2nd/17th fairway of the Old Course; the other is the Strathtyrum Course, which was constructed on part of the 118 acres of land which Mrs Cheape sold to the Links Trust in 1986 and which was opened for play in 1993.

THE STRATHS

The Strath brothers, Andrew, George and Davie, all made an important contribution to St Andrews golf, which was given recognition in the little Strath bunker which served the dual purpose of guarding the right-hand corner of the green at the short 11th and the left-hand approach to the seventh.

Andrew learned the art of clubmaking from Hugh Philp and Robert Forgan, and also served as a greenkeeper under Tom Morris on St Andrews Links. After spending a short time as keeper of the green at Musselburgh, he moved on to Prestwick in 1865 shortly after Tom Morris had returned to St Andrews. Andrew was an immediate success there and crowned his appointment by winning the 1865 Open Championship over what had become his 'home green'. But the Straths suffered from a hereditary affliction which claimed Andrew in his 33rd year in February 1868. He left a widow, a son and three daughters.

In the same year that Andrew died, Davie, aged 19, turned professional. Davie was never intended for the physically demanding game of professional golf, as it was in the mid-nineteenth century, and he was apprenticed as a law clerk in a local office. But with the family's health record, a life in the open air appeared to hold out better prospects for young Davie than a career in a dusty law office.

In 1868 Davie wanted to enter a professional competition for cash prizes subscribed to by members of the R&A, but some of the bona fide professionals protested that Davie was not 'readily on call for gentlemen players' and could not be considered a professional golfer. A meeting of the Subscribing Committee was called to consider the objection, and it was decided to give Davie a choice between declining to play as a professional, or, by playing in this competition as one, being regarded as a professional for ever. Davie threw in his lot with the professionals. The prize fund amounted to £20, allocated £8, £5, £4 and £3 – and Davie won none of it!

Davie Strath was a fine, stylish golfer, and in his day he was considered to be in the same rank as his great friend Tommy Morris; some considered that because of his smooth, elegant swing, he was a better golfer than the swashbuckling Tommy. He and Tommy figured in some splendid matches, both as partners and as adversaries, before Davie left St Andrews in February 1876 to become keeper of North Berwick Links. Later that year, he returned to St Andrews to take part in the Open Championship, and to suffer one of the greatest disappointments of his short but distinguished career. He had tied on a 36-hole aggregate of 176 with Bob Martin, but an objection was lodged that Davie had infringed the rules at the 17th by playing his shot to the green before the match in front had left it, his ball rolling against one of the party on the green.

The R&A did not immediately resolve the dispute but ordered a play-off for the following day. Davie argued that there was little point in having a play-off while a decision on a protest was pending, and he refused to play. Bob Martin therefore won the title on a walkover.

Davie's health, never stable at the best of times, began to deteriorate after this disappointment, and in September 1878 he sailed for Melbourne on a six-month health trip. It was no surprise to the people who knew him that Davie died as he reached Melbourne. Indeed, the state of his health was so precarious that until the day he sailed there was some doubt over whether he would be able to make the journey. Only because there was no chance of his surviving a winter at home was he allowed to leave. He was 29 when he died, leaving a widow and two children. It was reported that Davie's condition appeared stable for most of the voyage but before the ship reached Melbourne his health deteriorated to such an extent that he had to be stretchered ashore, and he died soon afterwards at the home of a friend.

The third of the Strath brothers, George, was never in the top rank of golfers, but he was a real craftsman among clubmakers. He became professional at Glasgow Golf Club and then moved to Troon in 1884. He was one of the pioneer Scots professionals who took the game to the United States. He went to Brooklyn, New York, and died in 1902.

ABOVE LEFT:
Davie Strath,
the youngest of
the three Strath
brothers, who died
on a health trip
to Australia, aged
29 (St Andrews
University)

ABOVE RIGHT:
Allan Robertson

ALLAN ROBERTSON

Some historians claim that Allan Robertson was the greatest golfer of his time, and that may well be so. But his influence on St Andrews and on golf in general goes much further than his prowess on the Links.

He was a club- and ballmaker of great repute, he was the mentor of Tom Morris, who was his junior by six years, and he has been revered by generations of golfers all over the world. Born in 1815, he is often referred to as 'the world's first professional golfer', but there must be reservations about this, for his grandfather, Peter Robertson, who died in 1803, was 'a ball maker and professional'.

He was never professional to the R&A, although he was called upon by the club in 1856 to put the course in order with particular reference to the greens. He may have been involved in the exercise of putting two holes on each green, thus giving rise to the pattern of double greens, for it is related elsewhere that at the May meeting of the club in 1857 the members enjoyed the innovation of two holes on each green.

Allan was also known as 'the Champion Golfer', although there was no championship event in his lifetime. Whether this was a self-styled title or whether it was thrust upon him is not clear; at least Allan never seems to have denied it, and it is recorded in stone on his graveside obelisk. The anomaly was noted by the members of Prestwick Golf Club, who decided that there ought to be a yardstick for deciding who was the champion golfer, and so the Open Golf Championship was born in the year after Allan's death.

As a golfer, he perfected the skill of iron play, particularly the running shot to the green. It is surprising that this should be so, for cleeks, or iron-headed clubs, did not become the norm on the Links until after the invention of the gutta ball in 1848, and Allan fiercely resisted the gutta for two years, as he saw it as a threat to his featherie-ballmaking business.

He had a genial disposition which endeared him to men of all ranks. Shortish, with a round, impish face, he was a popular partner for the gentlemen golfers of the R&A. His cordiality did not rest there but was extended to everyone who shared his interest in and love of the game of golf.

His untimely death came as a shock to the golfing world for, like his contemporary Tom Morris, he was a temperate man enjoying regular exercise over the Links and with scarcely a day's illness in his life. In the spring of 1859 he suffered an attack of jaundice; the infection never left his liver and he gradually sank, dying on 1 September 1859. Only a year before his death, he scored 79 on the Old Course, the first player ever to break 80.

On his death, the R&A passed the following resolution:

This meeting has heard with deep regret of the death of Allan Robertson, and they desire to record in their minutes the opinion universally entertained of the almost unrivalled skill with which he played the game of golf, combining a ready and correct judgement with most accurate execution. They desire also to express the sense of propriety of his whole conduct and unvarying civility with which he mingled with all classes of golfers; of his cordiality to those of his own; of his integrity and happy temper, and the anxiety he always manifested to promote the comfort of all who frequented the links.

The Union Club subscribed towards a pension for his wife, and clubs throughout the country were invited to contribute. St Andrews Golf Club, which Allan captained in 1853–4, was invited to accept Allan Robertson's locker, and for many years it was the privilege of the captain of the club to use the locker. Nowadays, it graces the club's foyer as one of its prized possessions.

Allan was laid to rest in the Cathedral Burying Ground, but his grave was undistinguished, and for some years it was merely a reference in the burial records. Ten years after Allan's death, this was rectified when the R&A set up a committee to provide a suitable memorial to Allan's memory.

Mr James Kirk, a local stonemason and sculptor, furnished a design for an obelisk six feet high. This involved an application to the Commissioners of HM Woods and Buildings, who were the custodians of the Burying Ground and who did not normally permit stones of this height to be erected. Permission was granted but with the proviso that 'a flagstone has to be placed on top of the remains'. In addition, a solid building was to be carried up to the base of the monument 'so that in all time coming, it remains the grave of Allan Robertson and no one else'.

The obelisk is set 25 yards west of the St Rule or Square Tower. The east face carries Allan's bust in bas-relief with the inscription: 'In memory of Allan Robertson, who died 1 September 1859 aged 44 years. He was greatly

The obelisk at Allan Robertson's graveside in the Cathedral Burying Ground. The inscription reads 'and for many years was distinguished as the champion golfer of Scotland'

esteemed for his personal worth and for many years was distinguished as the champion golfer of Scotland.' The north face has the game's insignia – crossed clubs and balls with the words 'Far and Sure'. The south face has the initials 'A.R.' enclosed in a wreath of laurel.

Allan had, for a time, another memorial – his own home at the corner of Golf Place and Links Road. During his lifetime, it was known simply as Allan's House, but in 1866, seven years after his death, the property came into the possession of a Mr Stobbie, who named the house Allan Villa.

The Robertson influence spread far beyond Scotland. Allan's brother David, having emigrated to Australia in 1848, did much to promote the game there. He was one of the founders of the Australian Golfing Society, which became the ruling body of the game in the Antipodes. It is interesting to recall that David sent home to Allan two nuggets of gold to be played for by members of St Andrews Golf Club during Allan's captaincy in 1854.

THE ANDERSONS

The patriarch of the Anderson family was David Anderson, better known as 'Old Daw', the man who organised the Ginger Beer Stall which gave the fourth hole its name. But Old Daw had other claims to fame – he was a club- and ballmaker, although it is true to say that he made few clubs and was not a serious contender in the field of clubmaking. He was the father of David, who founded the firm D. Anderson and Sons. David was a real craftsman, and he ran his firm successfully with the help of his five sons. Another of Daw's sons was Jamie, who, like Tommy Morris, won the Open Championship three years in succession – 1877, 1878 and 1879.

Daw was, until 1855, keeper of St Andrews Links, and he is credited with having cut two holes on the fifth green, originating the idea of double greens at St Andrews.

THE KIRKALDYS

Andra' Kirkaldy and Hugh Kirkaldy were well known on the St Andrews golfing scene, although they were not strictly home bred, their home being at Denhead, a few miles out of town. Hugh won the Open at St Andrews in 1891, but he died at the age of 29.

Andra' was less successful but better known. He was a completely different character from Hugh, restless and bursting with energy – at least in his younger days. As the years overtook him, restlessness gave way to impatience, an intolerance of fools and a dislike of petty authority. A fine, graceful golfer, he came close to winning the Open in 1889, when he tied at Musselburgh with Willie Park but was beaten in the play-off. Born in 1860, he showed early promise as a golfer, but his restlessness and quest for adventure led him to enlist in the Highland Light Infantry. This involved him in the Egyptian War and the bitter hand-to-hand fighting at Tel-el-Kebir, which quenched his thirst for adventure. After serving six years with the colours, he returned to St Andrews and the peace and quiet of the golf links to serve out his remaining six years with the Reserves. He ventured forth from St Andrews to be professional at Winchester, but after a short stay he returned to the place, and the language, he knew best. He was a Scotsman through and through, and he spoke the language most expressively. After the retiral of Tom Morris, Andra' was appointed honorary professional to the Royal and Ancient Golf Club. The duties were not onerous, but Andra' was proud of his association with the premier club and maintained a regular presence. On ordinary days, he would sit in the members' alfresco enclosure, casting a critical eye over the first tee swings, but on medal days he would sit as solid and impassive as the Rock of Gibraltar at the 18th green steps, rising as required to 'attend the pin' as the matches finished.

HRH the Duke of York (later King George VI) was captain of the R&A in 1930. Here he poses for a photograph with the club's honorary professional Andra' Kirkaldy

Andra' died in April 1934 at the age of 74. At his funeral, the Silver Club with silver golf balls attached was carried in the procession, an honour normally reserved only for past captains of the club dying in St Andrews.

ANDREW GREIG

After Tom Morris, the dominant figure on the Links was Andrew Greig, the official starter on the Old Course, who carried out his duties from a sort of box on wheels that could be moved as the teeing area was changed. It was probably one of the old Victorian bathing boxes used by lady bathers for undressing and dressing on the West Sands. A little hatch cut into the box about head height enabled the starter to communicate with golfers waiting to play. Andrew Greig carried out these duties from 1894, the date of the first of the Links Acts. His duties included the cutting of the grass in the first tee area, and he was engaged in this on the morning of 29 April 1915 when he collapsed and died.

Andrew Greig, starter on the Old Course, in his mobile 'office'

As starter on the Links, he was probably best known for his 'Fore', which was bellowed as a stentorian warning to stragglers crossing the Links by Granny Clark's Wynd. He was only 56 when he died but he had led a full and varied life. He learned his trade as a blacksmith in his native Kintore in Aberdeenshire, but, yearning for adventure, he joined the Royal Marines, serving them for the full span of 21 years. It was on his retiral from the service that he joined the Links staff. He had an impish sense of humour, and nothing delighted him more than to shout out the names of players which held a special incongruity, such as 'Playfair and Cheetham'. (Mr Playfair and Mr Cheetham were prominent members of the R&A who frequently played together.)

The story is told of a Frenchman who went to St Andrews to arrange a game of golf. This had to be done through Greig, who, in taking the applicant's particulars, asked his name.

'My name is Fouquier,' said the Frenchman.

'Ah weel,' replied Greig, 'when I cry oot Tamson and Tamson, juist you step onto the tee.'

Andrew Greig was a brother of Willie Greig, one of the best amateur golfers in Scotland. Willie was the first golfer to be captain of St Andrews Golf Club and the New Golf Club, as well as the first to employ a female caddie on the Links. He caused the golfing eyebrows to rise in 1913 when he played in the Amateur Championship with his daughter, Martha, as his caddie. There was never any probability of Martha buckling at the knees, for, great golfer as he was, Willie never had more than five clubs in his kit.

JIMMY ALEXANDER

One person who could match the stentorian 'Fore' of Andrew Greig was Jimmy Alexander, who took over as starter on the Old Course in 1919 and held the post for 39 years until his death in 1958.

Jimmy began his career on the Old Course in the old mobile wooden box from which Andrew Greig regulated the golfing traffic but within a few years he became the first occupant of the neat little office erected in the north-east corner of the first teeing-ground area.

At its best, Jimmy's 'Fore', directed at pedestrians crossing the first and 18th fairways, was startling and commanding, but his 'Play away, please', while imperative, was always courteous. His genial manner endeared him to all who visited the Old Course, and he had friends in many parts of the world.

A native St Andrean, he was a joiner by trade, but when the First World War broke out in 1914, Jimmy enlisted in the Black Watch, and lost his left hand in action on the Somme. On his return to civilian life, he worked for a short time as janitor at the local Burgh School before taking over as starter. Jimmy was an intelligent and articulate man, and he started more championships and professional tournaments than any other man of his era. He started seven Open Championships, six Walker Cup matches, four Amateur Championships, two Scottish Ladies' Championships, one British Ladies' Championship and several professional events.

Jimmy Alexander, starter on the Old Course, chats with A.F. Macfie, who at Hoylake in 1885 became the first Amateur champion

Despite his disability, he was a very competent golfer and a member of the One-Armed Golfers' Association. Many times, he calmed the nerves of a timid starter by hitting his first drive from the tee, and it was usually a good one, a score or so yards across the road. A gifted raconteur, he told many stories, some of them against himself. On one occasion, he recounted, he had momentarily dozed off, and he lifted his head to see a man swinging with a cleek at a ball about six inches in front of the tee markers. Jimmy left his office and told the player politely that iron-headed clubs were not to be used for driving from the first tee, that his ball was in front of the markers, and that it would assist him in playing the stroke if he set his ball on a wooden tee or a pinch of sand. The red-faced player spoke quietly to Jimmy: 'Will you get back into your box and let me play my second shot in peace.'

One of Jimmy's prized possessions was his autograph album signed by the world's best golfers, the captains of the R&A and members of the Royal Family. He had a wide variety of local interests, and, as well as his membership of St Andrews Golf Club and the New Golf Club, he was chairman of the local branch of the Black Watch Association and chairman of St Andrews United Football Club. Indeed, football and golf were his consuming passions, and he had friends at all levels of these games. If a ticket for a cup final or a Scotland v. England international was wanted, Jimmy knew where, and how, to get it.

During the Second World War, his disability debarred him from many activities, but he was enrolled as a warden in the Air Raid Precautions Service. As part of his contribution to the war effort, in the drive for scrap iron Jimmy amassed an enormous collection of iron club heads which were sent to him by golfers all over the country.

ST ANDREWS AND THE OPEN CHAMPIONSHIP

It was Jack Nicklaus who said that if a golfer is to be remembered he must win the Open at St Andrews. Many wonder why this should be so, for the Old Course is by no means the toughest course in the world. Probably the most important reason is the legend and the mystique which pervade the Links and have earned St Andrews the title the 'Home of Golf'. Some people tremble at the thought of playing St Andrews. There is the true story of an American serviceman on leave from Germany and keen to play the Old Course. A scratch player, he teamed up with a local club member who had a handicap in the high double figures. After easily winning the first three holes and having witnessed his hapless partner playing like a rank beginner, the St Andrean had serious doubts about the American's claim to play off scratch. His opponent, however, apologised for his play and explained that he was so tense with excitement at finally achieving his aim of playing the famous Links that he could not swing the club properly. Eventually, he relaxed and demonstrated that he was indeed a first-class golfer.

Bobby Locke putting on the 18th green of the Old Course to win the 1957 Open Championship. Some time later, Locke contacted the R&A, saying that he was certain that he had not replaced the ball on the correct spot after lifting to let his partner, Bruce Crampton of Australia, putt out (D.C. Thomson)

Kel Nagle and Roberto de Vicenzo putting out on the 18th green in the Centenary Open in 1960, when Nagle became champion (D.C. Thomson)

There is also the presence of the R&A looking majestically over the course like a golfing Big Brother and almost always the presence of a crowd of curious onlookers standing on the raised pathway behind the first tee. There are memories of the past, with Tom Morris's shop overlooking Old Tom's work of art – the 18th green – and the bas-relief head of the great man himself looking down from the west wall of the R&A Clubhouse.

There is also a unique mixture of antiquity and dignity with youth and vigour. The first come from the reminders of St Andrews' turbulent past, and the second from the students who study at the ancient university – the oldest in Scotland.

The natural arena formed by the houses in Links Road and Golf Place is unique among championship venues. People crowd the windows and sometimes the roofs to get a better view, and this is typical of the whole town's attitude to golf. The town eats, sleeps and lives golf. Ask any boy in St Andrews to turn out his pockets and the chances are that, in addition to the usual detritus, there will be a couple of tee pegs.

Joyce Wethered illustrated the town's obsession with golf when she told a story about her final match in the British Ladies' Championship against Glenna Collett in 1929. Joyce could not get the putts to go in over the first nine holes and was five down against Glenna, who had gone to the turn in thirty-four. According to Joyce, while the match was being played there was a stranger who was indifferent to golf strolling in the streets of St Andrews close to the cathedral and the university. The stranger was surprised to find himself addressed by a passing postman, in a depressed tone of voice, with the words, 'She's five doon.' Where else in Britain could such a brief but disconsolate monologue have been heard? Had the two strangers met an hour or two later, the postie might have quipped quite cheerfully, 'She's won three and one.'

While the Old Course may not be the severest test on the Open circuit, it does have its subtleties, and if the wind rises these subtleties can grow into massive problems. The huge double greens put a premium on good putting. The fifth and 13th greens, for example, extend in area to more than an acre. Boxer Sugar Ray Robinson said as he walked off the fifth green, 'That's the first time I ever had to pivot on a putt.'

There are other playful traps, such as the short 11th, with the green sloping from back to front. If a strong wind blows from the south-west, a downhill putt will never stop. Then there is the notorious 17th (Road) hole, which has dashed the chances of many an Open hopeful.

And finally the last hole. The tall, red sandstone Hamilton Hall behind the green makes distance assessment difficult, and even measurement charts can't help a player to judge the frolicsome wind currents which eddy around the famous finishing arena.

Firemen pump water out of the Valley of Sin in front of the 18th green following a cloudburst during the third round of the Centenary Open in July 1960 (D.C. Thomson)

WINNERS OF THE OPEN
AT ST ANDREWS

Until 1870, the Open Championship had been played exclusively at Prestwick. Thereafter, it was played over three courses, Prestwick, St Andrews and Musselburgh, the courses of the three clubs which contributed to the purchase of the new Open Championship trophy. St Andrews hosted its first Open in 1873.

The Old Course 1st and 18th holes, and the town at the end of the twentieth century (Masakuni Akiyama)

TOM KIDD (1873)

The first man to win the Open Championship at St Andrews was Tom Kidd, with a 36-hole aggregate of 179 against what was then a record entry of 26. His win halted the winning sequence of Tommy Morris, who had won the title four times in a row. Born almost with a golf club in his hand, Tom Kidd earned a reputation not only as the finest driver of a ball but also as a first-rate teacher of novices and adviser of experts. He was the first man to use ribbed irons to impart backspin to a ball. He was always known as 'Young' Tommy Kidd and, like so many brilliant exponents of the game in St Andrews, he was not allowed to grow old. He died on a cold January morning at his home in Rose Lane, St Andrews, in 1884 at the age of 36. He left a widow and two children.

Tom Kidd
(St Andrews
University)

In 1973, one hundred years after Tom Kidd's Open success, his great-grandson, Jim Kidd, flew to St Andrews from Montreal to celebrate the centenary of Tom's win, his intention being to better Tom's winning aggregate of 179. Jim, 39 years of age, made no claim to fame as a golfer, but he hoped that an easier course and modern equipment would help him to his objective. He scored 107 for the first 18 holes, which left him with the task of breaking 72 for the second 18. He did improve on his first round by scoring 95, for an aggregate of 202. Although he had failed in his mission, he promised to try again, saying he was 'getting to know the course better all the time'.

BOB MARTIN (1876 AND 1885)

Bob Martin won the Open twice over his home course. Noted for long hitting, he was also a perfectionist in the use of the cleek from all distances, especially in the run-up shot. His first win, in 1876 with an aggregate of 176, was a walk-over. He and young Davie Strath had tied on 176, but Davie had played his shot to the 17th green while the players in front were still putting, and the ball had trickled against one of the party on the green. A protest was lodged but the R&A, with uncharacteristic procrastination,

Bob Martin

Jamie Anderson

Bob Ferguson (St Andrews University)

Jack Burns

did not deal with it immediately but ordered a play-off the following day. Davie, who had worked in a local law office before turning professional, pointed to the futility of a play-off while a protest was still pending and he did not turn up. Bob Martin then won the title on the walkover. Honour was satisfied in 1885 when he won the championship with an aggregate of 171, beating 19-year-old Archie Simpson of Earlsferry by a single stroke.

JAMIE ANDERSON (1879)

Jamie Anderson, son of 'Old Daw', one of the great characters of the Links, won the third of his three consecutive wins at St Andrews in 1879, having won at Musselburgh with 160 in 1877, and at Prestwick with 157 in 1878. His winning score of 169 at St Andrews placed him ahead of Andra' Kirkaldy and Jamie Allan. He was not a spectacular player, but he was as steady as a rock and had a formidable reputation as a putter. His golfing strategy was to play steadily and let his opponent make the mistakes. He held professional appointments at Ardeer and Perth before returning to his native St Andrews. He died at Thornton, Fife, in 1905.

BOB FERGUSON (1882)

Like Jamie Anderson, Bob Ferguson also won the third of his three consecutive Opens at St Andrews, scoring 171. The Musselburgh man was the first non-St Andrean to win over the Old Course. He had earlier won over his home course in 1880 and at Prestwick in 1881 with 170. In 1883 he tied at 159 at Musselburgh with Willie Fernie of Dumfries but lost by a stroke on the play-off. He was a tenacious player; his game had power and accuracy and was untroubled by weather conditions – dry, wet or windy.

JACK BURNS (1888)

Jack Burns gave up his trade as a plasterer to become greenkeeper at Warwick, and when he won the Open at St Andrews with 171 he became the first Anglo-Scot to take the title. He beat the mercurial Ben Sayers on that occasion by one stroke. He was a swashbuckling player who delighted the discerning golfer. Yet his win in 1888 was accomplished in particularly difficult conditions, with a strong wind blowing from the north – conditions which might have seemed to favour the more conservative player. He was a highly respected teacher of the game with a great fund of patience.

HUGH KIRKALDY (1891)

Hugh Kirkaldy usually took second place to his better-known brother, Andra', in golfing terms, yet he achieved what Andra' never did – winning the Open. He had freedom and dash in his style with a full, fast swing which endeared him to the spectators. By the time he won the championship, he had scored 74 over the Old Course, beating Tommy Morris's 77, and within nine months he had lowered the record again to 73. The weather was stormy when he won the Open with two rounds of 83, for a total of 166, the best aggregate for the Open over the Old Course, beating Willie Fernie by two strokes. It was the last time the championship was contested over 36 holes. From 1892 onwards, it was played over 72 holes.

J.H. TAYLOR (1895 AND 1900)

J.H. Taylor was one of the 'great triumvirate' – Taylor, James Braid and Harry Vardon. He won the Open five times – twice at St Andrews and once each at Sandwich, Deal and Hoylake. He tied at Muirfield with Vardon in 1896 but was beaten in the 36-hole play-off. A native of north Devon, he learned his golf at Westward Ho!, and it was probably because of this that he was particularly reliable in windy conditions. He did much to improve the status of the professional golfer and was one of the founders of the PGA. His work to improve the lot of the professionals was recognised by the R&A, who in 1950 made him an honorary member of the club. He was a non-smoker and a teetotaller and lived to the ripe old age of 93.

JAMES BRAID (1905 AND 1910)

Like J.H. Taylor, James Braid won the Open five times – twice at St Andrews, in 1905 and 1910, twice at Muirfield, in 1901 and 1906, and at Prestwick in 1908. He was born in Elie, only a few miles from St Andrews, and learned his trade as a joiner. From there it was only a short step to becoming a clubmaker. He worked in his trade in London before turning professional in 1896. He held professional appointments at Romford and at Walton Heath, where he worked for 45 years and was an honorary member for 25 years. Braid was also made an honorary member of the R&A in 1950.

He worked with J.H. Taylor to found the PGA and, like Taylor, did much to improve the status of the professional game.

Hugh Kirkaldy

J.H. Taylor, pictured here with the cricketer Dr W.G. Grace (St Andrews University)

James Braid (St Andrews University)

Jock Hutchison, with the wooden railway bridge in the background (St Andrews University)

RIGHT:
Bobby Jones

FAR RIGHT:
Densmore Shute
(right) and Craig
Wood with the Open
Championship
trophy before the
1933 play-off,
which Shute won
(St Andrews
University)

In recognition of his legendary status in St Andrews, Bobby Jones was presented with the Freedom of the City in October 1958 when he was captaining the US team in the inaugural Eisenhower Trophy team championship for amateur golfers. Presenting him with the honour is Provost Robert Leonard (D.C. Thomson)

JOCK HUTCHISON (1921)

There is a touch of irony in Jock Hutchison's win in 1921, for he was born in St Andrews and learned his golf there. He emigrated to the United States and by 1921 had assumed US citizenship. His winning of the Open ushered in a 13-year period of American domination, broken only by Arthur Havers in 1923. In the run-up to the 1921 championship, Hutchison was not regarded as one of the likely contenders, for he had done little to make his mark in the top echelons of the game – and, indeed, did little after winning the title. Some commentators said he was lucky to win in 1921, and it is true that fortune smiled sweetly upon him. In the first round he holed his tee shot at the eighth, and his drive at the ninth lipped the hole but did not drop. Two holes in three strokes was a very important bonus, and he finished the round in 72. A third-round 79 saw him lose his lead, but a fourth-round 70 put him right back in contention. Hutchison had another stroke of luck in the third round. The amateur Roger Wethered walked forward of his ball at the 14th, and while walking backwards, eyeing the line of his shot, he trod on his ball and incurred a penalty. But for that penalty, he would have won the title. As it was, his final round of 71 gave him a tie with Hutchison on 296. In the play-off over 36 holes, Hutchison won by 9 strokes, 150 to 159. Although he had taken US citizenship, Hutchison never lost touch with his native town and visited regularly. The Jock Hutchison Cup is contested annually by members of St Andrews Golf Club.

R.T. (BOBBY) JONES (1927)

Bobby Jones has a special place in the hearts of St Andrews people. He won the Open three times – at Lytham in 1926 with 291, at St Andrews in 1927 with 285, and at Hoylake in 1930 with 291. His 1930 win was one corner of his Grand Slam – the Open, the Amateur, which he won at St Andrews, the US Open and the US Amateur. His first visit to St Andrews, in 1921, was not a happy one, for he was so disgusted with his score that he tore up his card. All was forgiven in 1927. The weather was good and the course was in prime condition. He had a first round 68 and led from start to finish. His aggregate of 285 – three below fours – was, in those days, extraordinary and established a new record for the championship. He was made an honorary member of the R&A in 1956, and when he returned to St Andrews in 1958 as captain of the US team in the inaugural match for the Eisenhower Trophy he was awarded the Freedom of the City. After his death in 1971, the tenth hole of the Old Course was named after him. A memorial extension of the organ was installed in the Holy Trinity Church, St Andrews, in 1974 and scholarships were set up in St Andrews University to exchange students with Bobby's alma mater in Georgia.

DENSMORE SHUTE (1933)

Denny Shute's win is notable, for it was the last in a long series of American wins. He was not the most distinguished of the American contingent in 1933. It was said that it was his defeat by Syd Easterbrook at Southport which cost the US team the Ryder Cup in that year. He, and Craig Wood who tied with him on 292, scraped through the qualifying stages with two strokes to spare. His progress through the championship attracted little attention, but it was astonishingly steady; his 292 comprised four rounds of 73. Walter Hagen's first round 68 and Willie Nolan's record-breaking 67 were not sustained, and Shute's 'straight-and-steady' policy brought him through. In the play-off over 36 holes, Craig Wood made a jittery start. He got into the Swilcan at the first and was bunkered at the second, taking sixes at each, allowing Shute to establish a four-stroke lead that proved decisive. His aggregate was 149, against Wood's 154.

RICHARD BURTON (1939)

Richard Burton of Sale in Cheshire was probably the unluckiest golfer ever to win the Open, for the Second World War was only weeks away and he missed the financial rewards which usually follow the title. The 1939 Open was tense right to the end. It was the year that Johnny Bulla burst onto the British golfing scene. Bulla's first-round 77 left him trailing far behind, but he followed this with 71, 71 and 73, and after four rounds he was in the lead with 292, and there was a shaking of heads that the claret jug was on its way back to the United States. Bill Shankland had a 25-foot putt on the last green to tie, but he missed; Reg Whitcombe, the defending champion, required 72 to tie but took 74. Finally, Dick Burton, needing 73 to tie, put in a nerve-tingling finish for a fourth-round 71 to win by two strokes.

SAM SNEAD (1946)

Sam Snead came to St Andrews in 1946 for the first post-war Open Championship with a moderate record. He had finished 11th at Carnoustie in 1937 and won the USPGA Championship in 1942 and the Canadian Open Championship in 1938, 1940 and 1941. Nevertheless, he had a reputation as a steady money-winner and was reckoned to have as good prospects as his compatriots Johnny Bulla, Joe Kirkwood and the great amateur Lawson Little. His prospects increased as the championship progressed, and after three rounds he was on a triple tie at 215 with Bulla and Dai Rees, with Henry Cotton breathing down their necks on 216. Bulla fell away in the final round with 79 to share second place with Bobby Locke at 292. Dai Rees fell

Richard Burton (D.C. Thomson)

Sam Snead receiving the Open Championship trophy (D.C. Thomson)

Peter Thomson

Bobby Locke (G.M. Cowie)

Kel Nagle (D.C. Thomson)

Tony Lema

LEFT: Jack Nicklaus receiving the Open Championship trophy in 1970 (D.C. Thomson)
RIGHT: Jack Nicklaus with the 1978 Open trophy

apart with 80 and Cotton could do no better than 79. Snead cruised round in 75 for 290 to win comfortably by four strokes. His personality could be a bit abrasive at times, and it was said that he felt his prize of £150 was so derisory that he gave it to his caddie. He proved to be no flash-in-the-pan champion, for he had a long and distinguished career in golf, and even in 1974, at the age of 62, he finished 3rd in the USPGA Championship.

PETER W. THOMSON (1955)

The Australian Peter Thomson was a great favourite at St Andrews, where he scored the second of his five Open successes. He won his first at Birkdale in 1954 and defended it successfully at St Andrews in 1955 and at Hoylake in 1956. He won his fourth at Lytham in 1958 and his fifth at Birkdale in 1965. It was at St Andrews that he met his colourful caddie Wallace (Guy) Gillespie, who shared some of his Open triumphs. In 1955 his first-round 71 left him two strokes behind the leaders, S.S. Scott and Eric Brown, but with rounds of 68 and 70 he edged into the lead with 209, one stroke ahead of Frank Jowle. His fourth-round 72 gave him a winning total of 281, two ahead of Johnny Fallon, who scored a brave fourth-round 70. Frank Jowle, however, was the man who made the biggest impression on St Andrews, for in one of the qualifying rounds he scored a fantastic 63 over the New Course, which one quick-witted golf writer headlined as A BIT OF A CHEEK BY JOWLE. Had the qualifying scores counted in the championship aggregate, Jowle would have been an easy winner.

A.D. (BOBBY) LOCKE (1957)

The 1957 Open was notable on at least two counts. First, it should have been played at Muirfield but because of the Suez crisis, which caused temporary petrol rationing, the venue was changed to St Andrews. It was Bobby Locke's fourth and last win in the Open Championship. Earlier, he had won at Sandwich in 1949, at Troon in 1950 and at Lytham in 1952. He led almost from start to finish, returning a first-round 69 that left him trailing Eric Brown by two strokes, which he wiped off with a third-round 68. His fourth-round 70 left him high and dry at 279, three strokes clear of Peter Thomson. But the drama did not finish with the holing of the last putt. When film of the final moments was screened, it was shown that on the 18th green of the final round Locke had marked his ball two putterheads from his fellow competitor's line. In replacing the ball, he failed to put it on the correct spot. The Championship Committee examined the incident and decided that, as he had derived no benefit, the result would be allowed to stand.

K.D.G. NAGLE (1960)

The Centenary Open was played at St Andrews in 1960 and was marred by a cloudburst which hit the course just as the third round was finishing. Manhole covers were thrown into the air by the upsurge of water in the drains, water rushed down the R&A steps like a cataract, and the hollow of the Valley of Sin was flooded in minutes. Kel Nagle, though well known in the southern hemisphere, had little track record in Britain before 1960, but he soon put an end to that. A first-round 69, then 67 followed by a third-round 71 put him in a commanding position. But the cloudburst had been so severe that the course could not be cleared in time for the final round, which was due to be played in the afternoon. It was played on the following day, when Arnold Palmer made a tremendous bid to catch him, scoring 68. But Palmer's aggregate of 279 left him just one stroke behind Nagle, who finished with 71 for 278.

TONY LEMA (1964)

Tony Lema's win in 1964 was remarkable, because he had never been to St Andrews before and had not played a full round over the Old Course before the championship began. His practice consisted of a few holes on the day before the championship opened. Arnold Palmer did not play in the 1964 Open, and perhaps that was a bit of luck for Lema because he was able to engage Palmer's caddie, Tip Anderson, for the big event. Tip described Lema as 'the most accurate driver of a ball I have ever served'. Lema was able to place his drives wherever advice led him, which is probably the best strategy for playing the Old Course. Lema was a talented golfer, and he proved it on the final hole of the last round. He was left with a shot of about 50 or 60 yards to the green, and most people expected him to loft it with a wedge to the green. But Lema played a low, running pitch as though he had known St Andrews all his life, and with a final round of 70 for an aggregate of 279 he won the title by five shots from Jack Nicklaus, whose final round of 68 could not atone for his first-round 76. Sadly, Tony and his wife, Betty, died two years later when a private aircraft in which they were travelling crashed on landing near Lansing in Illinois.

JACK NICKLAUS (1970 AND 1978)

Jack Nicklaus won the Open Championship three times — twice at St Andrews. His first win, in 1970, was memorable for Doug Sanders's disastrous mistake on the last green of the fourth and final round. Sanders had pitched to the green with his second and needed to get down in two putts to win the title. Unfortunately, he was on the top or right-hand side of the green, which left him with a downhill putt and an almost unpredictable borrow. He putted timidly, leaving the ball about two-and-a-half feet short, and he missed the next putt, scoring 73 to tie with Nicklaus at 283. The play-off was staged in a howling wind, with Sanders always playing catch-up. At the last hole, Nicklaus hit a mighty drive onto the green and holed out in two putts for a birdie three. Sanders matched his birdie but could not match his score, losing by 73 to 72. The 1970 Open was notable for the cloudburst which disrupted play in the first round. It happened in the early evening, and one of those still out on the course was the defending champion, Tony Jacklin. He had made a brilliant start to the defence of his title, streaking to the turn in 29. However, when the storm broke he cut his second shot at the fourteenth into an unplayable lie in the whins. When play was resumed the following morning, the magic had gone, although he did finish in a creditable 67. His final round of 76 left him three strokes adrift of the title.

Nicklaus won the title when it was next played at St Andrews, in 1978. Like his 1970 win, it ended a three-year spell in the golfing doldrums. Although his aggregate of 281 left him two strokes clear of his nearest challengers, he was hard pressed all the way. Simon Owen of New Zealand looked set to stake a claim to the title, but he overshot the 16th green, enabling Nicklaus to take what turned out to be a winning two-stroke lead. Tying with Owen for second place on 283 were three Americans: Ray Floyd, Tom Kite and Ben Crenshaw.

SEVERIANO BALLESTEROS (1984)

A curtain-raiser to the 1984 Open was a graduation ceremony in St Andrews University at which Jack Nicklaus was made an Honorary Doctor of Law (LLD) for his services to golf. This entitled him to be known as Doctor Jack Nicklaus.

The Open itself seemed to be going the way of Ian Baker-Finch, a 23-year-old Australian who had come to Britain with little reputation. He soon made one, for he held the outright lead for two days and went into the fourth round as joint leader. He made an unfortunate start to the final round, however, his pitch to the first hole spinning back off the green into the Swilcan Burn and laying the foundations for a disastrous final round of 79.

Nick Faldo, one of the British hopefuls, also faded from contention with 76 and by midday it seemed that the championship was developing into a three-horse race between Bernhard Langer, Tom Watson and Seve Ballesteros. Watson blasted his hopes at the notorious Road Hole (17th), overclubbing his second shot onto the road. Ballesteros and Langer walked to the 18th tee with the Spaniard holding a two-stroke lead. Seve played a fine approach to the last green and sank the putt to win with 276.

ABOVE LEFT:
Severiano Ballesteros
after holing the
winning putt in the
1984 Open

ABOVE RIGHT:
Nick Faldo
(D.C. Thomson)

NICK FALDO (1990)

The 1990 Open was played in the finest weather St Andrews had experienced that year, and unprecedented crowds flocked to the golf links for the final day's play. Unfortunately, the crowd got temporarily out of hand after Faldo and his playing partner, Ian Baker-Finch, had driven from the 18th tee. They broke from the sidelines and invaded the fairway, and Faldo had to sprint to keep ahead of the stampeding mass, who were only halted at the Valley of Sin by stewards and police. Fanny Sunesson, Nick's caddie, and Baker-Finch were 'rescued' from the crush before Faldo lined up his last putt. He had several shots in hand and holed out in 71 for a winning 270, five shots ahead of Mark McNulty and Payne Stewart, adding the Open title to the Masters which he had won earlier in the year.

JOHN DALY (1995)

St Andrews golfers have always admired the swashbuckling type of player, and in 1995 they got just that – and more – drama and emotion.

Wild man John Daly shared the lead after the first round and he held his position after the second. He seemed to have lost his chance after taking 73 in the third round. He had mastered buffeting winds in these early rounds and this surprised the knowledgeable galleries who had expected that his big hitting would get him into all sorts of trouble. He had also shown surprising delicacy in his pitching and putting. With one round to play, he was four strokes behind Michael Campbell who had surged to the front with a third round 65. The young New Zealander, however, scored 76 on the final circuit and Daly found himself in the clubhouse in the lead and with a nail-biting wait.

Costantino Rocca, a likeable Italian, was making a brave fight of it, but he seemed to have wrecked his chances when his approach to the notorious 17th ended up on the road. But he putted from the road and sank the four-foot putt for a par 4 to go within one shot of Daly's lead. He needed a birdie 3 at the 18th to tie. He hit a massive drive to within a few yards of the home green and then, to the horror of the huge crowd, he fluffed his pitch into the Valley of Sin. He studied the line of the putt carefully, but from his putting position in the Valley he couldn't see the hole. He hit the ball dead on target and when his caddie lifted the pin and gave a face-splitting grin, he knew the ball was in the hole for the

John Daly, winner of the Open 1995

most important birdie of his life. He had tied with Daly. He lay down on the green and beat the grass in a spontaneous surge of Latin exuberance.

The gallant Italian, however, had nothing in reserve after his nerve-tingling finish, and when the championship went to extra holes he was no match for the ice-cool Daly. The American underlined his superiority with a tram-ride of a putt at the second extra hole and it was virtually all over for Rocca. Daly, the USPGA champion of 1991, became the first United States winner of the Open since 1989 when Mark Calcavecchia took the claret jug to the States.

It was an emotional Open for Arnold Palmer, one of Britain's favourites, for it was his last Open Championship. There was a lump in many a throat when he stood on the ancient Swilcan Bridge and waved goodbye to the Old Course and the people of St Andrews.

TIGER WOODS (2000 AND 2005)

The Millennium Open lacked the cliffhanging drama of other Open Championships, for Tiger Woods won with a runaway margin of eight strokes.

But it provided the world with a display of golfing precision which will be difficult to match. It had been widely predicted that the young American prodigy would win – and win he did, with a modesty and humility rarely seen in one so young.

His 19 under par aggregate of 269 was a championship winner, and he was well on the way to gathering all four majors in the course of a single year. Some of the holes had been lengthened: new tees were laid down at the 3rd, 6th, 10th, 13th, 15th and 16th, adding about 200 yards and bringing the championship yardage to 7115. But Tiger's shot-making was so precise that not once on the rolling Links' fairways did he stray into a sandy hazard, all of which had been given extra teeth, with steeply revetted bulwarks.

Tiger Woods, Open Champion 2005 (Getty Images)

Bill Ritchie (left), Chairman of Trustees, with Sir Michael Bonallack beside him, presents the Freedom of the Links to Justin Leonard and John Daly

On the final day, Tiger was paired with his fellow countryman David Duval, whose golfing pedigree suggested that he was the only player remotely capable of making up the six strokes which was the gulf between them. Duval stuck manfully to his task but he dropped a shot at the 10th, then, when hope of a miracle was all but gone, his approach to the 17th finished in the dreaded Road Hole bunker. He squandered four shots there leaving second place in the championship to South Africa's Ernie Els, and third to Thomas Bjorn of Denmark.

As a curtain-raiser to the Millennium Open, a Past Champions' Challenge was played over four holes – 1st, 2nd, 17th and 18th – of the Old Course. Of the former champions, 22, led by 88-year-old Sam Snead, the 1946 winner, took part.

The winners were Tom Weiskopf, Tom Lehman and the reigning champion, Paul Lawrie, who received a cheque for £40,000 to be donated to the charities of their choice.

All who took part received a commemorative silver plaque and were given the Freedom of the Links.

If the Open in 2000 was significant because of the millennium and Tiger's runaway victory, the 2005 Open also had two events of enormous significance in golf. Tiger won again, at a canter, equalling Jack Nicklaus's achievement of back-to-back wins in St Andrews Opens 30 years earlier, and Nicklaus himself, now 65, bade farewell to tournament golf when he played his last competitive round at the 'Home of Golf'.

Whether by a masterstroke of organisation or pure serendipity, the R&A had arranged the starting times with the result that as Nicklaus was coming up the 18th fairway to an overwhelming reception, Woods was starting down the adjoining 1st fairway. The symbolism was clear to all – the torch had been passed to the younger man.

The enormous outpouring of affection for Nicklaus from the packed ranks all the way up and around the 18th touched the great man himself, who shed a tear or two, and also playing partner Tom Watson, who openly wept. The cheer when Nicklaus sank his birdie putt on the 18th green, to sign off the greatest career golf had yet seen, was almost earth-shattering. That he had chosen to play his last competitive round in the community which had rewarded him with an hononary degree from Scotland's oldest university, honorary membership of the Royal and Ancient Golf Club and honorary membership of the world's oldest artisan golf club, the St Andrews Golf Club, seemed entirely fitting.

That all took place on the Friday, leaving Saturday and Sunday for what seemed now to be the almost unemotional business of the championship, and for Woods to complete his domination of the rest of the field. He had started with a round of 66, leaving his competitors in no doubt as to his intentions, and by the end of play on Sunday the distance between him and the next man was five strokes. There had been a brief flurry of hope for a Scottish champion when Colin Montgomerie closed to within two shots halfway through the final round, but bogies at the 11th and 13th holes, with Woods birdying the 12th and 14th, signalled the widely expected Woods victory, won with a total of 274 strokes. Montgomerie finished in second place, his best Open finish by far.

Jack Nicklaus sends his final putt on its way into the hole to close his unparalleled career in tournament golf

V

STRIDING INTO THE
NEW CENTURY

CHANGE AND DEVELOPMENT

As the Links developed in the last decade of the twentieth century and the first decade of the twenty-first, comparisons could be drawn with a similar period of development a century earlier.

It had been in roughly the same 20-year span 100 years before that the last great burst of major development, both legal and physical, had taken place, accompanied at both times, perhaps unsurprisingly given the townspeople's strong feelings over 'their' Links, by some fierce controversies.

In the earlier period, the first Act of Parliament concerning the control and regulation of the Links had been passed. In the latter period, a change in local government in 1996 had almost resulted in the fall of the 1974 Act. The consequences of the latter would have been a loss of local control and a transfer of power to a large bureaucratic council in Glenrothes, where, it was considered, there was little feeling for the traditions of golf in St Andrews.

In the 1890s, the town was developing, railway excursions had started and visitors were flocking in, many wanting to try out golf and putting heavy pressure on the only course available at that time – the Old Course or, as it was then known, St Andrews Links. The response was to open three new courses: the New in 1895, the Jubilee in 1897 and the Eden in 1914.

A century later, the town's population had expanded and was continuing to do so, and there was another boom in golf tourism, but this time the tourists were coming by plane from all over the world specifically to play golf at St Andrews. The response was similar, with the opening of the Strathtyrum Course in 1993 and The Castle Course in 2008.

FINANCING THE LINKS

One major difference between the two periods was the financial situation. In the earlier period, with the Town Council in charge, there was little money for development. As a result, the R&A paid for the New Course, and the Jubilee Course was built on a shoestring by the Town Council for the princely sum of £178. In the late twentieth century and continuing into the twenty-first, the Links Trust capitalised on the boom in international golf tourism to fund a development programme for the Links costing in excess of £25 million over a twenty-year period – a sum undreamt of one hundred years earlier.

RIGHT: The timeless bridge over the Swilcan Burn. As well as golfers and sightseers, newly-weds have had their picture taken here – as long as it did not interfere with the golf!

Package deals: the Old Course Experience minibus outside the Links Clubhouse

To enable the programme to be financed, a contract had been entered into which sparked off one of the biggest controversies the Trust had yet to handle. The Trustees had considered many ways of raising the money needed to fill the black hole created by the necessary developments, but in the end they accepted a generous offer from the Keith Prowse organisation. The deal was that in return for a substantial premium the Trust would sell around 800 Old Course starting times each year to the company, enabling them to package these times up with local hotel accommodation, meals and transport. These packages would be sold under the trading name of 'The Old Course Experience' and would be aimed at the luxurious end of the market, primarily at corporate organisations and wealthy golfers worldwide. All the usual rules regarding reservations for the Old Course would apply under the terms of the new contract.

Local people were immediately on their guard. St Andreans felt that their rights and privileges on the Links were under threat, and they were afraid that the new deal might be to their disadvantage. It was, with hindsight, a fear of the unknown, and as the 'unknown' diminished, so did the fear. More importantly, faith in the integrity of the Links Trust was restored. Local golfers found that their privileged times were unaffected. Allocations to local golf clubs were unchanged, as were the starting times granted to local hotels and local tour operators. Some of the most vitriolic criticism came from distant tour operators around the world, whose concern was, presumably, a diminution of the profits from their own operations.

All the time, the Trust had been aware of the St Andrews tradition of low-cost golf for all – artisan or tycoon. They wanted to uphold that tradition, which had proved so attractive to the international tour operators, but extra money was required. By charging a premium to the new operator, the Trust was ensuring that at least part of that revenue would come back to the Links to finance the necessary improvements and developments. The tradition of low-cost golf remained for the local golfers and for all through the ballot, which was unaffected by the new arrangements. As the planned developments were primarily for the benefit of the visitors, it was probably only fair that the cost burden should fall on them.

How did the Trust use this additional money? As the Links had approached the twenty-first century, the Trustees had become increasingly concerned to ensure that any development was of high quality, something that had been difficult in the past as the Town Council had had little surplus to invest and was engaged in a perennial battle to keep local taxes down. The creation of the Links Trust in 1974, free from the constraints of using local taxpayers' money, and with a remit to manage the Links and nothing else, meant that any surpluses had to be reinvested in the Links and not used for other purposes. The Trustees were conscious that the visiting golfer, on whom the Links depended financially, had an almost limitless choice of high-quality alternatives in many different parts of the world. At the same time, modern communications had enabled the message that St Andrews Links was the 'Home of Golf' to be beamed across the globe, encouraging visitors to make the pilgrimage, and the Trustees wanted to ensure that the Links lived up to the billing.

When the agreement was made public, the Links Trust estimated that over a 10-year period it would generate more than £5 million in extra revenue. As it turned out, so successful was the contract that this estimate was exceeded, and Trustees decided to continue it for a further period.

THE FIRST WOMEN'S PROFESSIONAL EVENT

The first women's professional golf tournament came to the Links early in the new century in the shape of the 2007 Ricoh Women's British Open golf championship.

Although women had had equal access to the Links for centuries and many amateur events had taken place, there had never been a women's professional event. When it did happen, it was big: one of the four 'majors' in the increasingly popular world of women's golf.

Held over the Old Course in August, the championship attracted the top players from across the world, all vying to be the first-ever winner at St Andrews. The organisational arrangements made for this Open were

similar to those for the men's equivalent, and the R&A even made its locker-room facilities available to the women professionals. Attendance was over 60,000, leading to calls for a return to St Andrews as soon as possible.

The event was won by four shots by the world's number one female player, Mexican Lorena Ochoa, with a score of 287, five under par. In the first round she had set a new course record of 67 against the women's par of 73.

THE SHRINKING WORLD

St Andrews and the world had changed enormously in the century since the 1894 Act, and the Links had had to adapt to the changes while still retaining the characteristics for which it was so well known.

Global events had an increasing impact as the twenty-first century dawned, with two notable examples being the increase in use of the Internet and the terrorist attack on the World Trade Center in New York in 2001. While the first was beneficial, the effect of the latter on the Links was, unsurprisingly, a drop in visiting golfers in 2002, especially from the USA. No sooner had visitor numbers started to recover than there was a serious outbreak of foot-and-mouth disease in England, with dreadful television images shown around the world leading to another fall in the visiting golfers on which the Links depended.

St Andrews Links had been recognised for centuries as the Mecca of the game, and by the end of the twentieth century it was firmly entrenched as the fulcrum around which the international golf tourism industry in Scotland revolved. This meant that the Links had a growing economic role which was now not simply local but extended nationally across Scotland. This caused unease in some quarters of St Andrews, with the feeling that interests other than local ones were being given priority, but the Trustees remained conscious that the beneficiaries under the 1974 Act were to be residents of the town as well as the 'others resorting thereto' mentioned in the Act, and they continued to ensure fair treatment for both.

TOP LEFT: Lorena Ochoa's final putt on the 18th green

BOTTOM LEFT: The first Ricoh Women's British Open champion at St Andrews, Lorena Ochoa, insisted on having her photograph taken with the greenkeeping team

CENTENARIES AND CELEBRATIONS

The last years of the twentieth century saw the celebration of a number of anniversaries.

The opportunity, however, of marking the centenary of the volatile partnership between the Royal and Ancient Golf Club and the town of St Andrews was missed. It was on 20 July 1894 that the first of a series of Links Acts was given the Royal Assent. It was a Statutory Act that cemented an unlikely partnership which has endured, weathering a storm or two during its first century. The occasion went unmarked possibly because of the proximity of the 1995 Open Championship which was to be played over the Old Course.

But in 1995 the town, with the initiative of the Links Trust, celebrated.

THE CENTENARY OF THE NEW COURSE

The Royal and Ancient Golf Club was bound by the 1894 Links Act to lay out a second course, and this they did with commendable speed. The course was opened for play on 10 April 1895. This was the catalyst for names for the two courses. Until then, the Old Course was known simply as 'St Andrews Links', but with the opening of the second course they were distinguished by the simplest of expedients – the first course became the 'Old' course and the second the 'New' course.

Wielding the hickory: former Scottish Ladies champion and Links Trustee Marigold Speir drives off the 1st tee

214

To mark the centenary, a special tournament was held over the course on 9 April 1995 for local residents and members of golf clubs in the town. Many of the competitors turned up for play in Victorian costume. This touch of authenticity was enhanced by a rule of the competition that all players must use a hickory shafted driver to play from the first tee. They also had to use a hickory shafted putter throughout the round. A few played the whole round using only hickory shafted clubs. Each competitor received a commemorative medal. The New Course Centenary Trophy was won by sixteen-year-old Stuart Winter, a member of the New Golf Club. Other prize winners were: Ladies – Elaine Livingstone, Marigold Speir, Cynthia McDougall, Gwen Haines; Gentlemen – Yuille Bayley, Jim Davidson, Alex Maule, John Hair; Girl – Kathryn McCartney; Boy – Lee Rowan; Best Dressed – Lady – Eleanor Lawlor; Gentleman – Dick Hands; Best score with hickories – Barry Kerr.

Chairman of the Links Management Committee Robert Burns presents the 1st prize in the New Course Centenary Tournament to 16-year-old Stuart Winter (Ian Joy)

The tournament was followed by a dinner in Rusack's Hotel. Two years later – in 1997 – the Links Trust organised a series of events to mark 100 years of the Jubilee Course.

THE CENTENARY OF THE JUBILEE COURSE

The first Jubilee Course consisted of 12 holes and cost St Andrews Town Council £178 3s 8d. Even in 1897 that kind of money did not produce much of a golf course. It was basic but it was a place for children and other learners to play – out of sight and out of mind of serious golfers. It had been upgraded from time to time, principally in 1989 when Donald Steel's layout brought it to the championship standard predicted by Tom Morris's right-hand man, David Honeyman, and later by Willie Auchterlonie, the 1893 Open champion.

The Centenary Day – 22 June 1997 – was the apex of a programme of events spread over the summer. A handicap event for teams of four was held in variable weather conditions and the winning best-ball aggregate – 62 – was returned by Elaine Livingstone (St Regulus), Hamish Lohoar (St Andrews) and Chic Harper and Jim Galbraith (both St Andrews New). The first three teams received crystal goblets specially commissioned by the Royal and Ancient Golf Club.

The Men's Jubilee Centenary Open attracted a strong field from St Andrews and farther afield. Local players dominated, the first three scratch places being taken by St Andrews Club members J.F. McLeod, A. Donaldson and E. Graham. Leading handicap scorers were D. Pryde (Carnoustie) and M. Hopley (Baberton).

The ladies took over the course on 5 July when 62 clubs from all over the country took part in the Ladies' Centenary Open. Lesley Lloyd (Mount Ellen) with a net 74 won the principal award – a specially crafted brooch – while Elaine Moffat (St Regulus) won the scratch prize with 78.

The celebrations included competitions for Senior men and women and for boys and girls. Many of the events were so popular that they have become regular features on the golfing calendar.

Leaving golf clubs in the locker, the Links Trust decided that names should be given to the Jubilee holes, and with the co-operation of local newspaper the *St Andrews Citizen* the public was invited to submit suggestions. A panel of local people was appointed to judge the entries and choose the names. The event attracted wide interest and one of the names chosen was Playfair, recognising the work of Provost Sir Hugh Lyon Playfair. It had been submitted by Mr R.G. Palmer, an American. It became the name of the par 5 sixth hole.

The names chosen by the panel were: 1st Willie Auchterlonie; 2nd Whinny Knowe; 3rd The Skelp; 4th Crossgate; 5th Hackie's Barra; 6th Playfair; 7th Ayton; 8th Eden's Edge; 9th Windy Tap; 10th Spires; 11th Treble One; 12th The Butts; 13th Hale Bopp; 14th Willie Whitelaw; 15th Steel's Gem; 16th Freddie Tait; 17th Ladyhead; 18th Honeyman's Howe.

The Trust complemented this with a pictorial exhibition in the Links Clubhouse depicting life in the St Andrews community around 1897.

A homely touch was added to the celebration when the Jubilee Fountain was rescued from the anonymity of Kinburn Park, where it had languished for nearly 40 years, and installed near the first tee of the Jubilee. It had been inaugurated on the Bruce Embankment, near the Swilcan Burn, on the same day that the course was opened, marking the Diamond Jubilee of the reign of Queen Victoria. It was removed to Kinburn Park in 1960 to make way for hospitality tents of the Centenary Open Championship. Leading the restoration ceremony were members of the Trust and Management Committee along with Donald Macgregor, chairman of St Andrews Community Council, and Alastair Thake, a descendant of Provost and Mrs Macgregor who had performed the opening ceremony of the course one hundred years earlier.

TOP RIGHT: Winners of the Jubilee Centenary Day Competition

BOTTOM RIGHT: Unveiling of the Jubilee Fountain by Alastair Thake and Donald Macgregor, chairman of St Andrews Community Council

THE MILLENNIUM

To mark the coming of the millennium, the Links Trust organised two intertwined events, one local and one global. The local event was a competition involving 600 golfers teeing off simultaneously on all 99 holes of the Links in a shotgun start. It was called the Millennium Grand Match. The worldwide event was named the World Shotgun 2000 and involved 80,000 golfers from 557 clubs in 60 different countries taking their lead from St Andrews and teeing off at synchronised starting times on a single day.

Saturday, 24 June 2000 was the day chosen for both events as it was the longest day in the northern hemisphere, thus giving the maximum hours of daylight for the maximum number of golfers. Many months of precision planning came to fruition on that day, and the millennium was celebrated along with 600 years of golf at St Andrews Links. The event was launched at midnight in St Andrews with Old Tom Morris (David Joy) hitting the first ball from the first tee of the Old Course. This was shown on the Internet and was taken as the signal for players in the Far East to tee off. The second signal was given at 6 a.m. when the Royal and Ancient Golf Club's *Sutlej* cannon gave the order for players on the Old Course, already lined up at each of the 18 tees, to strike off. At midday the R&A gun was joined by two artillery pieces from the Highland Gunners. The blast was the signal for competitors on the 99 local holes to start and also for thousands of golfers in Europe and other countries as far apart as Russia and South Africa to do the same. The final call to action was given at 6 p.m. with another wave of golfers playing the Old Course. At the same time, enthusiasts in the Western Hemisphere were just beginning their day of celebration.

In St Andrews, 540 golfers took part over the five 18-hole courses playing Stableford with teams of 10, and 60 young players showed their skills over two circuits of the 9-hole Balgove Course.

The winning team was Mr Chippy's Club, 168 pts; 2nd was The Wanderers, 166 pts; and 3rd The Saturday Irregulars, 164 pts.

Members of the winning team each received a statuette of Old Tom Morris donated by Mr J. Neal Garland, a Texan businessman and a regular visitor to St Andrews, who flew over for the event and joined in the evening celebrations – a dinner dance in a marquee on Station Park just a pitch and putt from the Old Course, followed by a fireworks display. The youngsters on the Balgove Course were led home by Colin Mullins with 75. Iain Finlay and Christopher Seenan each scored 77.

Everyone who took part in the World Shotgun 2000 was given a certificate of participation signed by Sir Michael Bonallack, captain of the Royal and Ancient Golf Club, Bill Ritchie, chairman of St Andrews Links Trust, and Arnold Palmer, winner of seven majors.

Highlights of the event included holes in one by nine British golfers, and the auction on the Internet of the hickory shafted driver used by Old Tom Morris to start the celebration. It was a handmade replica of the play club used by Tom in 1885, crafted by Barry Kerr of Heritage Golf. The highest bidder was Ray Pershouse, Australia. The proceeds were divided between two charities – the Junior Golf Foundation and Keepers of the Green who provide powered mobility for the disabled.

BOBBY JONES CENTENARY

The centenary of the birth of Robert Trent Jones fell on St Patrick's Day, 17 March 2002. The closeness of the relationship between St Andrews and the greatest amateur golfer the world had ever seen meant that such an auspicious centenary could not be allowed to pass unnoticed in the town. The Links Trust decided to organise a celebration in two parts: a commemorative dinner and a golf tournament.

On Friday, 15 March, the Centenary Dinner, attended by 200 guests, was held in the Younger Hall on North Street, where, in 1958, Bobby Jones was presented with that rare award: the Freedom of the City of St Andrews. During the dinner, a film recording of the presentation was screened, allowing guests to see the ceremony and hear the words spoken by Jones that have now become so famous: 'I could take out of my life everything except my experiences at St Andrews and I would still have had a rich, full life.'

The five-course dinner was interspersed with speeches, first from John Imlay, former president of Jones's golf club, the Atlanta Athletic Club; then Bob Jones IV, Jones's grandson; followed by Sidney Matthews, a writer on Jones's life; and to finish, Sir Michael Bonallack, former captain and secretary of the R&A, and Britain's finest amateur golfer of the twentieth century. All of the speakers flew out to Atlanta the following day to participate in celebrations at Jones's home club.

On Sunday, 17 March, the Old Course was opened especially for the Bobby Jones Centenary Tournament. In a swirling haar, which drifted in from St Andrews Bay just as the tournament started, 100 golfers set off for a Stableford competition following a shotgun start at 11 a.m. The men's winner was Dr Duncan Lawrie, the chairman of the Links Trust, and the ladies' winner was Alma Robertson.

JUNIOR GOLF

The links at St Andrews have always been a golfing playground for the children of the town. They have been encouraged to take up the game through the provision of the nine-hole Balgove course, classes and competitions organised each summer by the St Andrews Children's Golf Club and a coaching programme introduced by the New Golf Club. Written into the 1974 Act is the requirement that residents' children aged 15 years and under – since extended to 16 – must be able to play free on all the courses, except the Old. The annual Boys' Open, held each August, dates back to the Second World War, and a younger sister was introduced in 1989 in the form of an annual Girls' tournament.

In 2001, however, the Trust was approached by Jim McArthur, a former captain of the New Golf Club, with the suggestion that there should be one organisation to coordinate all the golf coaching programmes related to children, as there were several different bodies each doing good but unconnected things. None had sufficient finance to do it comprehensively, and some of the people involved had had no training in how to teach and enthuse the children.

Future champions
(Masakuni Akiyama)

Youngsters on the
Balgove Course

Mr McArthur's suggestion was that the Trust should undertake the coordinating role, using the Links facilities, finance and people to set up the organisation to provide the comprehensive approach he considered desirable. After deliberating for a while over how best to take on the role, the Trust agreed – with the proviso that any new organisation should be controlled by a committee drawn from the local golf clubs as well as the Trust. It was felt that the project was very much a town initiative and should be seen as such.

Numerous meetings were held and, eventually, agreement with all parties was reached, with the result that St Andrews Links Junior Golf Association – SALJGA for short – was born. The aim was to provide children who joined with professional and semi-professional coaching from the age of five to eighteen, all at virtually no cost to the children or their parents. An army of willing volunteers recruited from the local golf clubs underwent a training programme designed to equip them with the knowledge and skills to teach the basics of the game to the next generation, and to provide the training required to meet all the child protection legislation which was now in place. Professional golfers were recruited locally to provide coaching at the more advanced skill levels, and the Trust was able to persuade golf equipment manufacturers to provide clubs for use by the budding golfers.

Finance to get the programme off the ground was found from an unusual source. Just at the time that SALJGA was being formed, the Old Course starter's box was being replaced. John Glover, a member of the Links Management Committee, suggested selling off the old one. This idea was

Youngers practice chipping on the Balgove Course, advised by one of the coaching volunteers

Five to seven year olds just starting on the road to success

seized on enthusiastically, and a plan was immediately put in place to hold an auction on the Trust's website. After a first, presumably frivolous, bid of five pounds from a tenement occupier in Glasgow, the final result was that sixty thousand pounds was generated from selling a building that had been intended for demolition, all of which went to help finance the programme. Further sums were obtained from a government sports promotion body and from the R&A. Additionally, the Trust contributed the coaching facilities and the people necessary to administer the operation.

In its first year, SALJGA coached over 500 young golfers, and over 100 adult volunteers underwent training in golf coaching. Six years on, the value of the programme could be seen in the number of SALJGA-trained youngsters challenging and often winning local, regional and national competitions. In particular, Ian Redford won the 2007 Scottish Under-16s title, Fraser Ogston won the 2004 Under-14s title and Ewan Scott won the 2007 Under-12s event. The programme's success was held up by sports promotion bodies as an example of how to imbue youngsters with the enthusiasm to take up the game and improve, and, equally importantly, to enjoy it.

SURFING FOR GOLF

St Andrews Links took its first step into cyberspace in 1996, obtaining a domain name, standrews.org.uk, and setting up a website to provide information to the rapidly growing number of golfers around the world who were becoming 'connected' to the Internet. At the time, few in the Trust realised the impact that this new communication medium would have, how it could be used, and how much benefit it could bring to golfers.

The first website was purely for information – on the courses, prices, history of the Links, how to book and facilities available. It was not long, however, before the next step – making actual bookings online – was being explored. This resulted in what was believed to be the first fully paid online golf booking in the world. It was made for play on the Jubilee Course in May 1998. The Links Management Committee had been tentative and very few times on this one course had been made available for online booking, but one of them suited a young Canadian researcher who worked in London and wanted to play at St Andrews with his father, who was coming to Scotland on holiday. The whole process worked smoothly, and to celebrate this 'first', they were greeted at the first tee with a glass of champagne.

Following that first hesitant step into the unknown of online booking, the Links Management Committee slowly relaxed, and ten years later times could be booked on the Castle, New, Eden, Jubilee and Strathtyrum courses. On some of the courses the proportion of total visitor rounds being booked online approached 20 per cent. The system was extended to local golfers as well, with times which were exclusively available to them able to be booked online.

The main Links information website was the subject of continuing development, and, as technology continued to race away, the Trust found other uses for this unique medium. In 2001, when plans were being put in place to extend the putting green next to the first tee of the Old Course, it was recognised that the existing starter's box would have to be scrapped and a new one built slightly further back towards the R&A clubhouse. Simply moving the existing one was not an option, as it did not meet the building regulations which would have to apply if it were to be moved. A new idea was suggested: instead of knocking it down and transporting it to the town tip, it could be sold.

RIGHT: A simple tick in the relevant boxes books a time on the Castle, New, Jubilee, Eden and Strathyrum courses

FAR RIGHT: The homepage of the St Andrews Links online booking system, Linksnet

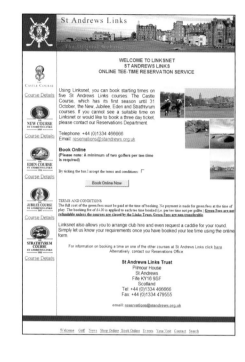

The Old Course starter's box raised almost £60,000 when auctioned on the Links' website

The tee plaque beside the 3rd hole of the Old Course, which was auctioned on the Links' website with the 17 other plaques to raise funds for junior golf

From there, it was only a short step to realising that this could be done by offering it for auction on the Links' website. Huge worldwide interest was generated and, as the deadline approached and the price went up, all but two bidders dropped out – one in California and one in Denmark – both keen to obtain the box for use on golf courses. The Californian succeeded with a last-second bid of almost £60,000. The windfall was put to good use in kick-starting the junior golf programme.

Following on from the success of the starter's box auction, when the tee plaques were being replaced on the Old Course the old ones were put up for auction in the same way, and a further £15,000 was raised for junior golf.

In the meantime, an online shop had been developed to provide a mechanism through which gift givers everywhere could obtain goods bearing the St Andrews Links and Old Course logos.

In 2006, the quest was started to find a name for the seventh course that was being built above Kinkell Braes. Up to then it had been referred to simply as 'course number seven'. A competition was launched on the Links' website enabling enthusiasts anywhere in the world to offer their naming suggestions. Over 4,000 were submitted, and the Trustees eventually decided that 'The Castle Course' was the most appropriate choice. This had been suggested by 14 different entrants. Their names went into a hat, and the lucky winner of the draw was Edwin Burtnett from faraway Florida.

HRH The Duke of
York congratulates
the opening drive
of Edwin Burtnett
from Florida, the
winner of the
competition to name
The Castle Course
(Alan Richardson)

Wholeheartedly embracing this new medium continued to be a success, and by 2008, usage of the Links' website, www.standrews.org.uk, was running at 12 million hits a month from an average of 50,000 users looking at 350,000 pages. In just a dozen years it had developed into an invaluable tool for golfers everywhere, as well as being an excellent way for the Trust to communicate directly with the world.

The short
17th hole on
The Castle Course
(Russell Kirk)

THE LINKS FACILITIES DEVELOP

THE GREENKEEPERS

Time was when chilling winds, in and out of season, whistled through the slatted ribs of the Black Sheds which were the primitive repository for the greenkeeping stocks, and the refuge where the score or so of outdoor staff unwrapped the cheese sandwiches and tea flasks which deputised for lunch.

That was away back in the 1950s. Before the new millennium was upon us, the greenkeeping staff had moved into spacious accommodation which had been put up – one, the Eden Greenkeeping Centre on the south side of the Links to service the Eden, Strathtyrum and Balgove courses and the Practice Centre; and the other, the Jubilee Greenkeeping Centre looking after the Old, New and Jubilee courses.

An early mowing machine makes its appearance on the Links, while the old method of cropping by sheep continues in the background

OVERLEAF: The last cut of the day: hand-cutting the 3rd green of the Old Course as the sun goes down (Iain McFarlane Lowe)

The machinery shed at the Jubilee Greenkeeping Centre has to accommodate the equipment, mowers, sprayers and tractors for three golf courses

RIGHT: Rebuilding the Principal's Nose bunker on the 16th hole of the Old Course

The Eden Centre, which cost £500,000, had 10,000 square feet of internal storage space for machinery and equipment and a small engineering workshop for minor maintenance. In addition, it had 2,500 square feet of external storage for top dressing and similar materials. The centre was opened in 1996 by Viscount Whitelaw in his capacity as president of the British and International Golf Greenkeepers Association.

Until the Eden Centre was in operation, all greenkeeping staff worked from maintenance sheds on the Jubilee Course. This meant that vehicles leaving the sheds to work on the Eden, Strathtyrum and Balgove courses had to cross the Old Course. The beneficial effect of the new centre on the turf of the Old Course was immediately obvious.

Shortly after the opening of the Eden Centre, work started on the new Jubilee Centre with a project cost of £900,000 – nearly double that of the Eden Centre; and it did have double the capacity. The old maintenance sheds at the Jubilee were demolished and work on the new centre began with design emphasis being focused on protection of the historic skyline.

The new centre was a magnified replica of the Eden Centre except that the engineering workshop was a fully equipped installation capable of undertaking the most complicated engineering rehabilitation and surgical

The slope in front of the 17th green of the Old Course receives close attention from the head greenkeeper, Gordon McKie

exercises on the highly technical greenkeeping equipment. The opening ceremony was performed in the spring of 1997 by the Scottish Office Minister Sam Galbraith.

Improvements in the greenkeeping facilities were long overdue, but there had simply been a lack of funds to do what was necessary. Now the new accommodation at St Andrews became the envy of the greenkeeping world.

For the new Castle Course, the buildings and facilities for the greenkeepers and their equipment were the latest and the best, leading the Sports Turf Research Institute's consultant to express the view that they were the best he had seen for a single course anywhere in the UK.

THE CADDIES

In 1995, a building used mainly as an office for the starter for the Bruce Embankment putting green, which lay beside the first fairway of the Old Course, was replaced with a structure twice the size of the original so that the caddies could be rehoused in larger and better conditions. The new building, however, was designed so much in keeping with the old one that many people commented that they could not see any difference.

The expansion had been necessary because the number of caddies was increasing as demand for their services continued to grow. The old building, behind the 18th green, had not provided facilities for the caddies as much as

The Ballot Master's office and public shelter in front of the R&A Clubhouse. It is still there today, but is now a Links shop

an office for the Caddie Manager. The new building, however, was equipped with toilets (both male and female), footbaths, a drying room and a large sitting room where the caddies could wait until called for duty. All this was a far cry from the open-air bench of days gone by.

The new caddie pavilion – calling it a caddie 'shack' did not seem appropriate

HALFWAY HOUSE

In the nineteenth century, Old Daw Anderson's Ginger Beer Stall provided on-course refreshment from his Victorian equivalent of the mobile catering van. Responding to requests from golfers, the service was reintroduced in 2001 when a specially designed van was driven onto the Links and positioned behind the 9th green of the Old Course. Here it was easily accessible to golfers on the New Course as well as the Old.

Providing hot and cold drinks, snacks and confectionery, the new service proved a popular move, although some golfers' expectations of beverages with a little more of a kick than tea, coffee and water were dashed. Liquor licensing laws had changed in the 150 years since Old Daw dispensed something a little stronger than ginger beer to those who asked.

INFORMATION TECHNOLOGY

The management of the Links at the turn of the century demanded modern systems, and that meant the development of an information technology system on a Links-wide basis. Soon there was no corner of the Links untouched by computer systems. Every starter's box, the caddie pavilion, the clubhouses, the shops, the greenkeepers' offices, the administrative offices and even the irrigation system were tied into computer systems, enabling staff to have accurate information, see at a glance what was happening and to take action accordingly.

STAFF TRAINING AND MANAGEMENT

As the pace of change had accelerated and the Links operation had expanded, managing the Links had become much more complicated, aided and abetted by a torrent of new legislation on employment, human rights, charities, equality, disability, health and safety, the environment, and accountancy standards, all of which affected the administration of the Links. This had led to a need for an increased volume and frequency of training, and also for specialist management.

Specialists in information technology, human resources, retailing, catering and communications had been brought in to ensure not only the efficient operation of these functions, but also that the never-ending flow of new legislation was complied with.

All these activities had seemed unnecessary just 20 years earlier, but now they necessitated much time and effort, all in addition to the traditionally accepted tasks involved in running the Links for golfers.

LICENSING AND RETAILING

In 1972 a Japanese commercial tycoon came to St Andrews to have a look at the Links and the Byre Theatre.

Zenya Hamada was passionately interested in the theatre but only financially interested in golf. He wanted to build, in Japan, a replica of the Old Course, and he was quite prepared to part with £100,000 for the privilege. He asked for a bagful of whin seeds to give his course an extra touch of authenticity and in return he gave the people of St Andrews hundreds of Japanese cherry tree saplings.

This happened before the passing of the 1974 Links Act, so the Links Trust was not involved. St Andrews Town Council who, at that time, owned the Links, gave Mr Hamada the permission which he had asked for because they believed that if he wanted to build a golf course similar to the Old, there was nothing to stop him. But they accepted the money with which Mr Hamada endowed a Trust 'for the benefit of golf and St Andrews'. The Hamada Trust was still in existence 40 years later. Mr Hamada's action was quite unsolicited, and at the time, it did not occur to St Andrews Town Council that there was a crock of gold at the end of 600 years of golfing history. Perhaps local government constraints prevented the Town Council from exploiting this horn of plenty, but when the Links Trust was created these obstacles did not apply and an agreement was struck with a Japanese company which wanted to use the Trust's logo on its merchandise. It was a huge success for the Trust and, obviously, for the Japanese entrepreneur.

To build on this, the Trust used two limited companies: St Andrews Links Limited and St Andrews Links Golf Shops Limited. The first company was to licence the Links logo and trademarks on a worldwide scale, and the second was to handle the retailing. The separate companies were necessary to protect the Trust's charitable status.

These activities caused no wear and tear on the courses, so any profits would be a bonus to the Links. Both companies covenanted their profits to the Trust, which then had to invest them in the same way as surpluses from golf operations in the improvement of the Links.

In the mid-1990s, with the advent of computer games based on golf, licensing income really took off, with a variety of game producers, usually based in the USA or Japan, vying to be licensed to use the Old

Course in their games. More than £1.5 million of additional revenue was lodged in the Trust's bank account in the ten years leading up to 2006 from companies such as Nintendo, Sega, Microsoft and Electronic Arts. Meanwhile, the original Japanese licensee continued to send in a steady stream of remittances, and other smaller licence arrangements added to this beneficial flow.

The Trust's retailing operation had started in 1989, through a retail franchisee, in one half of the small building behind the 18th green of the Old Course. This building had fulfilled several functions in its long life. It had been built in the early twentieth century as the 'The Ballot Master's Box'. The principal duty of the occupant was to supervise the form filling by applicants for starting times on the Old Course, to make the draw and to distribute ballot sheets to their various vantage points throughout the town. The Town Council was a bit nervous about the building in view of the 1879 judgement in the Links 'Road Case' in which their Lordships declared that 'the Magistrates are not entitled to alienate any ground of this description but must hold it for the use and enjoyment of the community of the burgh'. To meet this point, and to settle their nerves, the Council built a verandah on three sides and installed form-fitting bench seats all around it so that it could be designated a public shelter.

When the caddie shelter, including the Caddie Master's office, in the north-east corner of the Flagstaff area was demolished, the Caddie Master moved in with the Ballot Master and the east side of the 'Box' was turned into a caddie shelter.

In 1949 Lord Brabazon introduced the caddie cart to the Old Course and caddies almost disappeared. The Ballot Master had long since become redundant and his duties fell upon the Caddie Master. Now it was the Caddie Master's turn to go, and his duties were inherited by the Old Course starter. This left the building unoccupied – but not for long. Winnie McAndrew, wife of Jock, who had been running the Golf School on the North Haugh, took a lease of the building and started hiring out caddie carts, and golf clubs and selling other golfing minutiae.

When the McAndrew family retired in 1989, the Trust decided to use it as their own shop, although the eastern half continued to be used as a caddie shelter until 1996, when the caddies moved into their new pavilion beside the first fairway of the Old Course.

The retail franchising arrangement continued until 1999, when the contract came to an end and St Andrews Links Golf Shops Limited came into being to run the retailing in-house. By then there was already a successful shop in the new Links Clubhouse and a much smaller one planned for the Eden Clubhouse. The latter proved unsuccessful and

was soon closed. Under the new company, sales and profits increased rapidly. The extra funds generated were soon a major contributor to the Trust's total income, easing the financial pressures created by the Links development programme.

St Andrews Links Golf Shop behind the 18th green of the Old Course

In 2005, the R&A approached the Trust to see if its retail company had any interest in taking over the large shop the club owned in Links Road, overlooking the 18th green of the Old Course. In 2001, the R&A had bought the whole of the property owned by the St Andrews Woollen Mill – a property which had previously housed the Forgan golf factory – to use as additional club premises and offices. The ground floor, however, had been retained as a retail outlet and been leased out, but the lessee now wanted to relinquish the lease.

The size of the premises, even after the R&A had reduced it by deciding to use some of the space for its equipment-testing operations, was more than four times the total existing retail space then used by the Trust's company. Accepting the offer would be a big step, but it was decided to take on the challenge, and the new shop started operations in 2006. It was called simply The Old Course Shop and it offered a much wider range of products than the existing outlets, with high-quality brands such as Ralph Lauren, Burberry, Bobby Jones and Dunhill all featured.

The Old Course
Shop in Links Road

The creation of The Castle Course offered another opportunity for the Trust's retail company to spread its wings through the opening of an outlet in the clubhouse there. This took the total number of shops to four, but this new outlet was different as it sold only products bearing The Castle Course logo.

The new operations prospered, as did the new Internet shop, helping to provide the Trust with firmer financial foundations.

The course guide
cover shows The
Castle Course logo: a
knight's helmet taken
from the Monny-
penny coat of arms,
the family which,
in the Middle Ages,
owned the area where
the course is built

CHRONOLOGY

1457   Golf forbidden by Act of Scottish Parliament (James II).

1471   Ban repeated (James III).

1491   Ban repeated (James IV).

1502   James IV takes up golf and buys his first golf clubs.

1552   Archbishop John Hamilton given permission by the burgh to establish a rabbit warren on the Links. The charter confirms the rights of townspeople to play golf over the Links.

1583   Two St Andrews boys rebuked by Kirk Session for golfing on Sabbath.

1611   Archbishop Gladstanes grants a contract confirming Hamilton's charter.

1614   Gladstanes grants a charter confirming his contract.

1620   James VI grants a charter ratifying Gladstanes' contract and charter.

1726   William Gib granted permission to put rabbits on the Links, with a proviso that the golfing area must not be damaged.

1754   Society of St Andrews Golfers founded.

1764   Standard round of golf stabilised at 18 holes.

1769   Exchange of land between Laird of Strathtyrum and Town Council, with a condition that the golfing area is not to be ploughed up or enclosed.

1771   Fees of caddies fixed.

1797   St Andrews Town Council reported to be in financial difficulty. Robert Gourlay and John Gunn advance money to the Town Council on the security of the Links.
Gourlay and Gunn exercise their right to sell the Links by disposing of part of the land to Thomas Erskine of Cambo.

1799   Links sold to Charles and Cathcart Dempster, who introduce rabbits on a commercial scale.

1801   George Cheape, captain of the Society of St Andrews Golfers, complains that rabbits are destroying the Links.

1805   Court of Session decides that inhabitants of St Andrews have the right to kill and destroy rabbits on the Links, and the Rabbit Wars begin.

1817	Thistle Golf Club founded.
1821	James Cheape of Strathtyrum buys the Links and brings the Rabbit Wars to an end.
1834	Society of St Andrews Golfers becomes Royal and Ancient Golf Club of St Andrews.
1842	Sir Hugh Lyon Playfair elected provost of St Andrews.
1843	St Andrews Golf Club founded.
1848	George Cheape redeems the feu duty on the Links for £1,000. The gutta ball is invented in St Andrews by Robert Adams Paterson.
1850	Tom Morris's first son, Tom, dies aged four (April).
1851	Young Tom Morris born (20 April). Old Tom moves to Prestwick.
1852	St Andrews branch railway line opened.
1853	R&A and Union Club unite.
1854	R&A Clubhouse built.
1856	Sir Hugh Lyon Playfair appointed captain of R&A. Two holes cut on each green of Old Course.
1857	R&A spring meeting approves cutting of two holes on each green.
1859	Allan Robertson dies aged 44 (1 September).
1864	Tom Morris returns from Prestwick. Andrew Strath moves to Prestwick.
1865	Tom Morris takes over as custodian of the Links.
1866	Tom Morris sets up his own club- and ballmaking business.
1867	Ladies' Golf Club formed.
1868	Andrew Strath dies at Prestwick; Davie Strath turns professional. Rose Golf Club formed.
1869	A bunker disappears from the Old Course and is then reinstated and named Sutherland. Evening classes for caddies begin. Improvements at Links Road and approaches to Old Course. Eighteenth fairway returfed. Memorial to Allan Robertson erected in Cathedral Burying Ground.
1870	New green created west of Swilcan Burn, enabling the Old Course to be played on left- or right-hand circuits.
1872	R&A Clubhouse extended.
1873	Tom Kidd wins first ever Open over Old Course.
1875	Tommy Morris's wife dies in childbirth (11 September). Tommy Morris dies (25 December).
1876	Davie Strath leaves St Andrews to be keeper of the Links at North Berwick.

Davie Strath ties for Open at St Andrews but loses on a technicality.

Tom Morris's wife, Agnes, dies (1 November).

1878 Memorial to Tommy Morris unveiled in Cathedral Burying Ground (24 September).

Davie Strath dies on a health trip to Australia.

1880 The Links Road War.

1893 St Andrews Town Council sets up a committee to examine golfing facilities on the Links.

R&A appoints a committee to confer with James Cheape with a view to purchasing the Links.

Dr Thomas Thornton advises Town Council to seek parliamentary authority to acquire the Links.

Town Council offer £4,500 for the Links; R&A offer £5,000.

James Cheape sells the Links to R&A.

Town Council petitions Parliament for power to acquire the Links.

George Bruce plans Bruce Embankment reclamation.

Jack Morris, youngest son of Tom Morris, dies (22 February).

1894 St Andrews Links Bill goes before Scottish Select Committee.

Town Council and R&A tell Select Committee that agreement has been reached between them.

St Andrews Links Act 1894 receives the Royal Assent (20 July).

James Cheape asks for compensation for loss of pre-emption rights.

Andrew Greig appointed starter at Old Course.

1895 New Course opened for play.

Rusack's chimney built.

1896 James Cheape's pre-emption claims settled and feu disposition between Town Council and R&A formally signed.

First rules for caddies approved by Town Council.

1897 Jubilee Course opened (22 June) – 12 holes.

1902 New Golf Club founded.

1903 David Honeyman, Tom Morris's henchman, dies (7 June).

Sheriff of Fife approves bye-laws for caddies.

Tom Morris retires as custodian of the Links.

1904 Andra' Kirkaldy prosecuted for caddying.

Caddies' shelter erected behind 18th green of Old Course.

Death of Robert Adams Paterson, inventor of gutta ball.

1905 Jubilee Course extended to 18 holes.

St Andrews Golf Club buys a clubhouse.

1906 Tom Morris's third son, Jamie, dies.

1907 R&A build a shelter at first tee of New Course.

Planting of whin bushes on sand dunes at Jubilee Course.

1908   Tom Morris dies after an accident in New Golf Club (24 May).

1912   Rumours that R&A might leave St Andrews.

Proposals for a new Provisional Order the subject of a plebiscite.

1913   1913 Links Act receives the Royal Assent (10 July).

James Cheape leases land to Town Council for fourth (Eden) course.

H.S. Colt commissioned to design Eden Course.

1914   Eden Course formally opened (4 July) with first match between a local team and a team of R&A members.

1915   Links gets its own water supply from Cairnsmill.

St Andrews Town Council begins formation of West Sands Road by controlled refuse dumping.

Andrew Greig, starter at Old Course, dies (29 April).

1919   Jimmy Alexander appointed starter at Old Course.

1920   Eden Tournament inaugurated.

1923   Granny Clark's Wynd gets a tarmac facelift.

1924   1924 Links Act receives the Royal Assent (29 May).

1931   Championship Committee proposes gate money as a means of regulating crowds.

1932   1932 Links Act receives the Royal Assent (16 June).

1934   Andra' Kirkaldy dies (April).

1936   James Cheape sells part of Eden Course to Town Council.

1938   Proposals for adapting New Course to become a new super-championship course.

Willie Auchterlonie authorised to supervise reconstruction of Jubilee Course.

1941   Air Cadets Parkinson and Tulip play first legalised Sunday golf over Eden Course.

1945   R&A admits difficulty in meeting its commitments to the courses.

Local plebiscite favours Sunday golf on Eden Course.

1946   Tribunal meets in Edinburgh (26 and 27 July) to consider Town Council's petition to Parliament.

Links Act receives the Royal Assent, abolishing the St Andrews citizens' right to free golf (19 December).

Reconstructed Jubilee Course opened (1 June).

1949   Hull's bunker on 15th fairway of Old Course filled in.

Lord Brabazon introduces the caddie cart to Old Course.

1953   Town Council and R&A discuss the club's financial difficulties.

Agreement between council and R&A to set up a Joint Links Committee for the control and management of all courses.

1958   Death of Jimmy Alexander, starter at Old Course.

1963 Town Council reviews conditions of 1953 Agreement and decides that there should be no change.

1964 Town Council commissions Hawtree Report.

1965 Reservation fees introduced.
Hawtree Report submitted with proposals for redeveloping New and Jubilee courses.

1966 Town Council agrees Alcan Tournament to be played at St Andrews in 1967.
Town Council and Championship Committee agree that gate money limits be removed.
Estimates approved for changing-room complex to serve New and Jubilee courses.
Old Course Hotel built.

1967 1967 Links Act receives the Royal Assent (14 July).
Overhead irrigation system installed on Old Course.

1969 St Andrews–Leuchars railway line closed.
Wheatley report published on Local Government Reform in Scotland.
Car parking provided on Bruce Embankment.

1970 Local golf clubs join with R&A in seeking to retain control and management of the Links within the town.

1971 R&A issue a Memorandum (27 May) outlining their proposals for control and management by establishing a Links Trust.
Town Council agrees (11 August) to seek power to establish a Links Trust and Management Committee.
Irrigation system installed on Eden, New and Jubilee courses.
Land acquired from Strathtyrum Estate to form Balgove Course.

1972 Tenth hole of Old Course named 'Bobby Jones' (10 September).

1973 Mr C.D. Lawrie submits proposals for redesigning Eden Course.
Plans for changing-rooms behind the 18th green of Old Course considered and rejected; Bruce Embankment site considered and rejected.

1974 1974 Links Act receives the Royal Assent (10 April).
Links Trust rejects the C.D. Lawrie proposals on the advice of St Andrews Town Council.

1981 Links Trust acquires Rusacks Hotel.

1983 Starting and finishing areas of Jubilee Course designated a 'Practice Area' during major events.
Links Trust agrees Jubilee Course be upgraded to championship status.
Links Trust seeks 20 acres of land from Strathtyrum Estate for practice facilities.

1985	Links Trust sells Rusacks Hotel to Trust House Forte.
1986	Mrs Gladys Cheape agrees to sell 118 acres of Strathtyrum land to Links Trust.
	Architects commissioned to produce plans for development of newly acquired land and contiguous areas of the Links.
1987	Links Trust approves plans for reconstruction of Eden Course.
	Water supply from Cairnsmill under review and a storage reservoir provided near Jubilee Course.
	Borehole sunk on North Haugh.
1988	Plan for changing-rooms beside Himalayas rejected.
1989	Upgraded Jubilee Course formally opened by Curtis Strange.
	Reconstructed Eden Course opened with free transport service for course users.
1990	Links Trust acquires Pilmour Cottage from owners of Old Course Hotel in exchange for a 99-year lease of ground between 18th green of Eden Course and the old pavilion.
	Free transport service for Eden Course users withdrawn due to lack of demand.
	Links Trust announces development plan for the recently acquired land.
	Links Trust decides to convey water directly from borehole to pumping station.
1992	Links Trust buys out all the significant Strathtyrum rights.
	Extensive consultations by Links Trust on proposed Links Clubhouse sited west of the Himalayas for all golfers playing the Old, New and Jubilee courses. Plans significantly revised and submitted for planning permission.
1993	Planning permission for clubhouse obtained from North East Fife District Council.
	Redesigned nine-hole Balgove Course opened.
	Golf Practice Centre officially opened by Catriona Lambert and Strathtyrum Course formally opened for play on the same day (1 July).
1994	Building of clubhouse begins (January).
1995	St Andrews Links Clubhouse opened.
	New Course Centenary celebrated (April).
	Arnold Palmer says 'goodbye' to St Andrews.
	Links Trust announces package deal with Keith Prowse.
1996	Ownership of Links transferred to Fife Council.
	St Andrews Links on Internet.
	Eden Greenkeeping Centre opened by Viscount Whitelaw.
1997	Jubilee Course Centenary celebrated (June–July).
	Jubilee holes named.
	Jubilee fountain installed near 1st tee.

Jubilee Greenkeeping Centre opened by Sam Galbraith, Scottish Executive Minister.

1998 Fife Council drop plans to review 1974 Links Act.
Website redesigned.
Trustees decide to to seek land for seventh course.

1999 First phase of new irrigation system completed.
Cost of fighting erosion doubled and planning permission sought for further defensive action.
Silver Jubilee of creation of Links Trust and Management Committee.

2000 Millennium celebrated with the World Shotgun 2000 and the Millennium Grand Match (June).
Past Open Champions granted Freedom of the Links.
Tiger Woods wins his first Open at St Andrews.
Planning permission granted for measures against coastal erosion.
Eden Clubhouse opened by Menzies Campbell.

2001 Second phase of new irrigation system completed.
Study course for caddies inaugurated.
St Andrews Links Junior Golf Association (SALJGA) formed.
Old Course's starter's box auctioned on Links' website.
Sand replenishment of beach defences in Eden Estuary.
On-course refreshment reintroduced after 150 years.
Website redesigned.

2002 Option to purchase land for seventh course agreed with landowners.
Bobby Jones Centenary celebrated.

2004 Strathtyrum Course medal tees introduced, adding 500 yards.
Planning approval given for seventh course.

2005 Construction of driving range extension starts.
Construction of seventh course starts.
Jack Nicklaus plays final competitive round.
Tiger Woods wins his second Open at St Andrews.

2006 Competition to name seventh course runs on Links' website.
Driving range extension opens.
The Old Course Shop opens.

2007 First women's professional event played over the Old Course.
Lorena Ochoa wins the Ricoh Women's British Open at St Andrews.

2008 The Castle Course opened by HRH The Duke of York.
Sand replenishment of beach defences in Eden Estuary.
The Curtis Cup is staged on the Old Course for the first time and is won by the American team.

INDEX

OVERLEAF: The third green of the Castle Course
(Russell Kirk)